Georgia
of the
Jungle

Georgia Egge

TATE PUBLISHING, LLC

Published in the United States of America
By TATE PUBLISHING, LLC
All rights reserved.
Do not duplicate without permission.

All Scripture references are King James Version,
unless otherwise indicated.

Book Design by TATE PUBLISHING, LLC.

Printed in the United States of America by
TATE PUBLISHING, LLC
127 East Trade Center Terrace
Mustang, OK 73064
(888) 361-9473

Publisher's Cataloging in Publication

Egge, Georgia

Georgia of the Jungle/Georgia Egge

Originally published in Mustang,OK:TATE PUBLISHING:2004

1. Christianity 2. Biography

ISBN 0-9748244-7-X $13.95

Copyright 2004

First Printing: May 2004

It would not be possible to write this book without the help of my husband, Dennis. He has given me much support and patience as I undertook this project. I appreciate him for all the ways that he shows me how important this book is for the extension of the Kingdom of God. We worked together in many areas of bringing this book to its completion and I am truly grateful that God has blessed me with such a husband.

I also want to thank all those who helped me with the computer skills I needed. Without these people, this book could not have been done in such a short time.

Thank you to all those who were an encouragement to me giving me the additional strength to realize the potential that was in me. Without the prayer support and financial support of these special friends, the task would have been much more of a challenge.

To God be the glory for the privilege to serve Him. Without the Lord Jesus, and the revelation of the Holy Spirit teaching me how to go forward in victory, there would be no book. The ministry that I have is only because of the work that the Holy Spirit has done in me. I love Him will all my heart and my desire is to see salvation and freedom come to every one who will call on His name and believe that He gives life more abundantly as one surrenders to Him.

- Georgia Egge

The following pages will take you on a journey with Georgia Egge around the world. Listed below are the places you will read about that she traveled to preaching the gospel of Christ to thousands:

Mexico
- Summer/87
- Summer/88
- Summer/89
- Summer/90

Costa Rica
- 6/90

Guatemala
- 1/6/91–1/19/91
- 2/16/92–2/28/92
- 1/5/93–1/18/93
- 11/15/93–11/29/93
- 1/3/94–1/28/94

Ecuador
- 4/13/93–5//6/93
- 6/7/94 -/6/22/94
- 5/31/97
- 3/22/00–4/15/00

Peru
- 1/18/95–2/14/95
- 6/6/95–7/4/95
- 11/25/95–12/11/95
- 3/23/96–4/20/96
- 11/18/96–12/13/96
- 5/5/97–6/17/97
- 10/26/98–11/23/98
- 2/1/00–4/00
- 10/23/01–11/18/01
- 1/31/03–3/28/03

CHAPTER 1

Childhood Dreams

IGH IN A TREE sitting in my tree house dreaming of far away places, I spent so many summer days back in the 50's when I was a kid. I was a tomboy at heart and very much at home on our small, Minnesota farm. The farm was surrounded by thick groves of trees and underbrush; the kind one could hide in without being disturbed. The summers were short because of being so far north. Every chance I could I would be working on some ingenious way to create an atmosphere of adventure. I could imagine that I was an explorer on expeditions to dangerous places where every movement around me provided intrigue and surprise. Sometimes I was an archeologist digging up buried treasure fully expecting to find what no one had known was there. There were ponds to cross on homemade rafts that always seemed to falter before reaching the other side. The ponds were never deep enough to worry about drowning. I had not learned how to swim yet so they were not particularly threatening to me.

Whatever my imagination could conger up would take me into many hours of exciting and exhilarating adventure. I now think back to those days and realize I was sort of a combination of Indiana Jones, MacIver, and Crocodile Dundee all rolled into one.

Always I was keeping my eye open for anything that could be nailed together or tied together to create a way to have an adventure. My family had thrown out many wonderful pieces of junk over the years. There actually was an old dump down in those trees. I spent time after time combing through the rubble knowing that I would soon discover exactly what would take me on my next adventure.

I loved to climb every tree that was strong enough to support me. It did not matter if they were skinny or fat. There was a natural climbing ability built into me by God that had to conquer every tree on the farm. I especially liked to find a very high tree with a good view. One could see things in a much different perspective being high in a tree. I guess it all figures because now I only want to see things from a heavenly perspective as God would see them. I realized that the only way to really know what life was all about was to see it through God's eyes. He had created me for a special purpose and it was in my heart from the beginning. It is so interesting how God lines everything up in our lives to flow with the calling He has given us. I often spent long hours sitting in that tree house I had made of scrap lumber and old, discarded pieces of tin. My mind tried to figure out why I was on this earth and what would the future hold for me.

It was so much fun to climb up on high buildings and structures. There was a challenge even in that. The windmill stood so stately and lofty in the middle of the farm. It always invited me to come up higher and view the countryside. Now and then, one of my parents would catch me and yell at me to get down before I fell and hurt myself or even worse. A roof, of course, I thought was there for someone to climb onto and jump off of. My bedroom was on the second story and the porch roof was just outside my window. It was high, but not high enough so I could not jump from it. I used to do just that when the traditional method of walking out the door seemed just too easy. My parents really didn't understand the adventure in me. Even to this day, they cringe every time I say I am returning to the jungle. To them it is a place that just maybe would not let me come back alive. I tried to understand, but try as I may, I simply could not see anything but an adventure to be had.

I loved to be around the water and in Minnesota it is said that there are 10,000 lakes. I believe it is true. Being on the farm presented some problems because I lived miles away from my friends in town. I had my adventures on the farm, but the ones that lived in the town had a nice, big lake to swim in, sidewalks to roller skate on, and parks to play in. I spent time with them in the town and my friends spent time with me on the farm. It seemed like a way for everyone to have a balanced time of recreation and fun.

I especially wanted to learn how to swim, but it was very hard to get to town for regular swimming lessons. Sometimes my mother would let me go to the lake and spend time enjoying the water. There were lifeguards on duty and what could happen? I knew she did not want me to go into water that was over my head since I did not know how to swim. Oh, how I wished I could swim! There was no other way to learn except to just get into deep water. I watched those who could swim and I practiced the strokes that they were doing. Little by little it seemed with great effort I could get from one place to another. Now, this lake had two big rafts in it that one could dive from. They were in water that was way over my head. The lifeguards would sit in their rowboats keeping their eyes peeled for anyone in trouble. As I got a little older, my mother trusted me to the lifeguards and went downtown to do her shopping. This was my chance to be adventurous. If I could just get from shallow water to the first raft, I could rest and then go on to the second. It was a plan and I was able to swim in an awkward sort of way to conquer this challenge in front of me. I was so pleased that I accomplished such feats and felt very comfortable in water too deep for me from that time on. Somehow, I would learn to be a good swimmer and enjoy the wonderful lakes that were around me. I had an ability to float with no effort. It seemed my body was built in such a way that it would not sink. This gave me great security as I taught myself to swim and I had no fear, yet I had enough sense to not go beyond my limits of strength.

CHAPTER 2

Impressions

IREMEMBER WHEN we first got a TV set and it fascinated me to see those black and white programs. My favorite thing to watch was Tarzan of the Jungle. I was so interested in the jungle for some reason. I loved the suspense and the primitive surroundings of it all. I dreamed of being Jane and having such adventure as she. I watched programs where there were volcanoes erupting and dinosaurs roaming the landscape. The primitive cultures seemed to draw me to them somehow. I watched intently as people coped with their environments and surmounted all the dangers around them.

These beginning impressions of the jungle and primitive cultures were causing a desire to rise in my heart. I had no idea where such a place or people were, but I always wanted to know. Such were the early years of my life down on a farm in Waseca, Minnesota.

As I grew older, I continued to keep my bent for adventure. My school days were fairly uneventful, and I was not particularly fond of having to go to school. Some subjects were hard for me, and some were very easy. Some subjects I liked, and others I did not.

One of the subjects that I really liked was Latin. It seemed challenging to me and it made sense in so many ways. It actually helped me understand English grammar better. In my final year of high school I took a Spanish class. That was it! I loved studying this language, and I realized that Latin helped me with the grammatical structures in it.

I learned about the culture of these Latin people living in a continent not so far away. I longed to go to Latin America and help the people there. I did not study about the jungles of South America or Central America so I did not realize they were there. The books and movies were mostly about the bigger cities and tourist attractions, but not jungles.

When I graduated from high school, I went on to a college that was on the other side of the state. I wanted to study Latin and Spanish. There were not too many colleges in the vicinity of where I lived that offered Latin as a major, so I was limited to basically two or three choices. I decided on a private college in Moorhead, Minnesota just 300 miles away.

Learning Time

Now, I was a churchgoer at this time in my life, but I really did not understand what having a personal relationship with Jesus Christ meant. I did not realize that all these things that I desired in my heart were put there by God. Without an understanding of God's leading in my life, I still somehow stayed in His will and purpose for my life. Now I am not saying that I was not a little rebellious in those days. I was an adventurer remember, and I loved to take a dare and do something challenging. I am sure that God had angels stationed all around me to keep me safe from all the predicaments I got myself into. Indeed, I lived life to the fullest that I could without creating too much havoc.

It was in this time of my life that I met who was to be my husband for all these years. His name was Dennis, and he was nothing like me at all. There was an irresistible drawing to him that I could not explain. We met on a blind date arranged by a roommate of his in another university in the area called NDSU. It was so romantic, and I will never forget that night. We dated, and as time passed it seemed that he was causing me to settle down and see life in a more mature way. Neither he nor I knew that our futures would be knit together in the plan of God. It was less than two years later that we were married. He was off to work in a small town in North Dakota for the university that he had attended. I reluctantly went to such a small place. Little did I know that for the next 30 years of my life, I would be in North Dakota. Our family began to grow, and soon we had three children and all of life and adventure to far away places was put on hold. Actually, I forgot all about those childhood dreams that I had had back in my tree house.

In college I was preparing to be a Spanish and/or Latin teacher. Finishing the remainder of my education had to wait since there were no universities in small towns under 1,000 people. I was not very thrilled to be living in such small places, but again God was watching over me. When a crisis would arise in my life and I did not know what to do, I would pray to God for help. It seemed He did not hear. I was troubled and needed a friend to talk to. God always sets us up it seems and has the answer right in front of us. He sent a new pastor and his wife who had a little girl the same age as our little girl to the community. We met each other and began to get acquainted as time went on. In my desperation to have peace with God in my crisis time, I called this pastor's wife to come and talk to me. I was not one for discussing my problems with people, but I was in turmoil with my emotions. She listened to me ever so intently and then, just as simply as can be, she introduced me personally to Jesus Christ who is the Prince of Peace. What a wonderful peace came into my life that day as I surrendered myself to Him. It truly was a day that changed me in so many ways. My husband saw a new wife emerge from this encounter with Jesus. It was hard to explain, but I had a new heart and new desires to be pleasing to the Lord. I started going to Bible Studies and then church, and Dennis came too. Together we took our family to church and became very faithful to the Christian life. We met so many wonderful Christian people at the church, and from then on we wanted to be involved with the Lord's work.

After a few years, my husband received a promotion and we moved to a bigger city called Minot where I could finish my education. I had to change my major from Spanish to Physical Education. There was no major in Spanish at that university at that time. The kids were almost all in school and I became a very busy mom. I studied hard and took care of duties around the house. Plus, I was involved with community projects and the children's school activities. I knew that God was giving me a special energy to keep it all going.

As the years wore on and the kids were in high school, I basically forgot about studying Spanish. I stayed involved with the family, church and community activities. I even tried my hand at selling Real Estate, which went very well. I still liked to have a challenge. My husband would tell people, "Just tell her she can't do it and she will find a way to do it." But, as you can imagine, I could not continually be so busy, and do a good job keeping up my commitments. Eventually, I was falling apart from all the pressures and did not know what to do. I was going to church and praying, but it just seemed like that was not helping. I had friends who seemed to be very happy and joyful. It seemed like they were really excited and "on fire" for God. My spiritual life certainly needed a boost because I was having a struggle. I wanted to know where to find this joy and excitement in God.

New Beginnings

They told me about a little church that was having revival meetings, and I wanted to go. I drove myself to this church that I had never heard of before, not knowing what to expect. I was fairly religious, but I just knew there was more to living a Christian life than going to church. On the way to the church that night in May of 1979, I prayed to God telling Him that my life would be completely His and I would trust Him and do whatever He wanted me to do. That night God met me and took me at my word. I received a touch in my spirit like never before, and I knew that God had done a deeper work in me. I had a hunger and desire that was so intense for His Word and to know Him intimately in my spirit. I had cried for three days in my discouragement preceding this encounter and now I was so full of joy because Jesus had set me free. I prayed with an intercession that came from down deep in my spirit and I spoke with a spiritual language that I had never heard before. I knew that new life had filled me with great hope and joy and a zeal for the Lord Himself was very evident to me and those who knew me. I had an intense longing to study the Word of God, and soon revelation and insight seemed to open up to me. I began to see spiritual gifts operating in my life, the ones that are mentioned in I Corinthians 12. It was something supernatural and I knew that God was the author of these signs and wonders.

With my hunger for God growing each day, I wondered where a church would be that would allow this new life in me to flourish. Some churches did not understand this Pentecost experience that I had received. I prayed and God brought others who also had received this baptism of the Spirit. The Holy Spirit was sovereignly falling on believers from many different denominations all around the country, and churches began to arise out of small groups gathering to pray and worship together. There was a freedom that we had never had before in church. The Holy Spirit used ordinary people to do extraordinary things. We saw many healings and miracles happen and knew that it was a new day for the church.

Life is not without its problems, and the process leading to growth and maturity is not always pleasant. But, God has a divine plan and purpose for everything that we pass through. Little by little, I was beginning to see that I must obey the Word of God if I wanted to follow Him. I went to many conferences and heard many wonderful speakers share truth from the Word. I sat on the edge of my seat absorbing the Word like a sponge. There were so many questions that I had, and God always seemed to answer them just when I needed the answer.

I met many wonderful pastors and prophets who spoke into my life. The word they shared always seemed to confirm the longings in my heart. They spoke of other countries and much ministry in days to come. They talked about starting churches and counseling others and sharing the Word of God in our home and abroad. I was so hungry for the knowledge and understanding of the Scriptures that I read and devoured them every single day. I knew that this was God Himself speaking to me. I worshiped the

Lord with my guitar in my simple sort of way, and God even gave me new songs from my spirit that He inspired. I knew that God was leading me on to fulfill the prophetic word He had spoken to me. There was an assurance that it really would come to pass, but I did not know how it could happen.

What I want to share with all of you reading this book is God is a God who will sovereignly guide you every step of the way into your destiny. There is nothing or no one who will hinder you from finding that destiny except you. There are no limitations in the supernatural realm of the Spirit, but there are many in the natural world of humanity. God requires a willing heart, faithfulness and obedience to His Word. He has already walked out your entire future and He knows everything that every day of your life will hold for you. He allots His sufficient grace to you each day and only asks that you yield yourself to it and allow Him to divinely enable you to do what He has required.

When I understood that it was His calling on my life and His divine enablement, it made life ever so much more endurable.

You see, He always asks more of you than you can give Him in your natural ability. He is so pleased when He can reveal Himself to you in so many wonderful and opportune ways. He loves to see you step out in faith and trust only in His ability to accomplish what He asks you to do.

As you meditate on what you just have read, humble yourself unto Him and pray this prayer with me:

My precious Father, I do not understand all that you have required of me, but this day I surrender my will to you and give you permission to lead me into the purposes you have ordained for me to walk in. I want to serve you with all of my heart and find increased love in my devotion to you. Reveal yourself to me in the quietness of my spirit and fill me with new joy and appreciation of your will working in my life. Guide my every footstep in your paths of righteousness and truth as I follow you into an adventure that will fill my life with reverence and awe of your overwhelming grace and love. I will give you all the glory. Amen.

14

CHAPTER 3

Lessons Of Grace

OD ALLOWED ME to have a couple of years of getting "unbusy" so He could change me and transition me to make me more flexible and yielded. I had mellowed out quite a bit, I thought, and yet the dealings of God were present to cause me to be even more obedient. Many misunderstandings came as I was being broken and humbled by the Holy Spirit. I felt that those times when God was certainly bringing me into my ministry areas, were times when I just had to stand by faith knowing that God had it all under control. After all, I had promised Him that He could have full control of my life. I felt much rejection from my friends who did not realize the toll the humbling processes of the Holy Spirit were having on me. I knew that I must strive to keep my outlook on life good and my attitudes godly. Those days were days when I would intercede before the Lord and ask Him to transform my character into something with which He would be pleased. I studied the Word and worked hard to apply God's grace to my everyday life. It seemed like I would come apart at the seams sometimes, but God always assured me that He was doing a good work in me. I learned to stand on every word of God to get through my emotional "roller coaster" rides. My every thought had to be brought into subjection to what God wanted and not what my flesh cried out for. When I believed the truth of God's Word, the truth set me free. It was how to stay free that was the real challenge. But, then I was always up for a challenge.

I loved to go to Bible camps up in the prairies of Canada, which was not too far from where we lived in North Dakota. I was so excited to stay in my tent or in a rustic cabin during the week-long camp meeting. I especially loved to "rough it." My family also enjoyed these times, especially the children. I truly felt that their lives would have never been the same without those times with the people of God in a camp environment. There were so many children their ages and they made life long friends from those camps. They were all filled with the Holy Spirit in the camp meetings and I saw them have a hunger for a close relationship with God. The gifts of the Spirit even started to operate in their lives.

Those camp times were so wonderful, and I will never be able to thank God enough for allowing me to attend them. My husband, Dennis, enjoyed these times too, but he was not quite as enthusiastic as I was. He would take his own amount of time to evaluate all those new things that God was doing by His Spirit. He was a very conservative man and I respected that, but I knew I must be at those meetings! I remember having to beg him some-times to go to those camp meetings because He wasn't quite sure what God was doing. My persistence usually paid off, and we would get to camp every year. I was so caught up in my own spir-itual hunger that I became a little insensitive to his needing to hear from God for himself. As a wife and being of a strong spirit, I used my best arguments to persuade my husband to do things my way. He would not always permit this, but in most cases I was tri-umphant! Of course, God was doing something in all of us through those camp meetings even under duress.

I remember one year in the late 80's about the time to reg-ister for camp. As usual I geared up for all my best persuasive arguments of why we had to go to camp. This time was different. I really did not want to have my way, but my will was very strong. I longed to go to camp and learn from the tremendous speakers who would come. The spiritual hunger in me would not be abated. I had been praying for my husband that he actually would take a strong spiritual headship in the family, and that he would be the one to suggest that we go to camp or any other spiritual function. I knew that I must decrease so he could increase. Now, that was much easier said than done. How defiant the flesh can be when it does not get its way!

That night as we were getting ready for bed, I pressured him about camp. He said we were not going, and he would not budge in his decision. Try as I might, I could not change his mind. Needless to say, my flesh did not like that at all! The flesh, being what it was, sent me off in a huff to sleep in the basement. When I speak of flesh, I am referring to my own stubborn will. A strong willed person is a challenge even for God, I thought! Deep down inside I knew that the day had come to give in to the Holy Spirit and not justify things anymore. God wanted a change in my behavior and I had no more options if I wanted to see my husband grow spiritually. I knew God was right and I would now have to struggle with my emotions that wanted to feel rejected and hurt. Spiritual warfare began to arise in my spirit against my unsurrendered will. I determined to let the Holy Spirit have his way with me and come to a place of rest and peace, accepting the fact that I was not going to camp that year. I also asked God to give me more love and respect for my husband for making a decision and sticking to it. It took all the reserve grace of God that was due me that night to bring myself through to victory so I could go to sleep with a clear conscience. I remember that I was just on the verge of falling asleep, when the flesh and my will to overcome and have my way, rose up in me again. I understood what Jacob must have felt when he wrestled with the angel. The account is recorded in Genesis 33:24 in the Bible.

The whole process of yielding my desire to go to camp and to love and respect my husband even more for standing up to me began anew in my soul. I knew that Jacob even had to have the strong area in his body put out of joint to allow God to "break him." How incredibly strong the will is, but the spirit must prevail and obey the will of the Lord. Another battle brought me to a certain place of brokenness and I knew that this time, the Holy Spirit truly had won. I felt the presence of the Lord in the room in such a sweet, special way and knew that I had won a major victory for the Lord. There was a peace in my spirit that could only come from total surrender to the will of God. I knew then that the only way to win was to allow the Holy Spirit to crucify my fleshly desires.

As I was drifting off to sleep, I felt someone touching me on my shoulder. It was Dennis, and he came to tell me that God had awakened him from sleep and clearly showed him that he was to take us all to camp that year. Oh, the rejoicing that filled my soul! That night God was on the throne and I never will forget the lesson I learned. When I got out of the way, Dennis heard from the Lord for himself. I knew that my name had changed as did Jacob's. I knew I would surrender my will to God's. This was significant of a character adjustment that only can come from obeying the will of God and denying the flesh to ever desire its own way. That night the love of God overwhelmed both my husband and me, and we grew closer together in the knitting of our spirits. Unity does not come easy, but it is the willingness of surrender that brings the greatest joy. How will the Spirit of the Lord be victorious in my life? It will happen by choosing to deny my flesh and yielding to his grace in total obedience.

Stretching Time

I have learned that God works in my life in different ways to bring me through the dealings of dying to the flesh. Sometimes He will cause me to have a major breaking such as the one I went through. Following this are many smaller breakings that are less traumatic, because the flesh does not have the power it once had. At other times, He allows many smaller breakings and then a major dealing and final blow to the strongest areas of my flesh. There are combinations of smaller and more severe dealings happening in repeated patterns as He matures me. God is looking for a people who will be so surrendered to Him that He can do as He pleases and use them in any way He chooses.

I have many times been stretched in my faith and trust in the Lord. These times of stretching, I believe, will never end until I go to be with Him in eternity. I have realized that God is interested in revealing himself to me and to others as the God of the impossible. He will do what I cannot do if I would be willing and obedient to cooperate with Him. After all, it is that He receive all the glory and not me.

What I want to share with you in the following examples is to encourage you to trust the Lord, and not lean to your own understanding, nor tell God that you are not qualified, and therefore, cannot obey. The very thing that you cannot do is what will qualify you to do more of what you cannot do!

God is a God of grace that is sufficient in time of need. This is his divine enabling to do something that you do not have the ability to do in your natural strength.

As I stated before, I received a degree from college and changed my major from Spanish to Physical Education because there was no Spanish major at the college I was able to attend. There were about twenty years from the time I had taken my last Spanish class in the 60's until the 80's. Spanish was all but forgotten to me, and the only taste of it that I received was substituting in the public school system in Minot, North Dakota where we lived. I substituted in various subjects as the need arose. I enjoyed teaching on a part time basis while my children were in school. I even substituted in their classes from time to time. They prayed, I know, that I would not embarrass them in any way! I am sure you know what I am talking about. Parents also prayed that the children did not embarrass them in any way. Somehow we all managed to get through those child-rearing years intact by the grace of God.

One year in the late 80's, a shortage arose in the school system for a Spanish teacher. The superintendent looked high and low for someone who would teach three classes of Spanish and a couple of hours of another subject that there was a need for. No one could be found. I had a degree in Physical Education and a minor in Spanish but had never had practical training in teaching Spanish. I enjoyed substituting in all the various subjects in the junior high and high schools in the Minot area and had no intention to teach full time. The administrative staff knew who I was and who our children were because of the activities and participation we enjoyed with the school system. I was happy to have my freedom to work at my leisure, and the church that we were a part of starting kept me involved in its related activities. I loved to lead Bible Studies and see ladies grow in the Lord. This church was very open to the moving of the Holy Spirit and had a good connection with a church in Canada, which did much for my spiritual growth in those days. I had learned much wisdom from the mistakes I had made along the way and from the revelation of the Word of God. I had a fear of God in me that told me to always obey what He wanted and not do my own will, no matter what it cost me. It was that very understanding that gave me wisdom that would keep me on course with the purposes of God.

Our two oldest children, Laurie and Darin, were in high school by this time and the youngest, Shannon, was just finishing elementary school. We accepted various exchange students from Spanish speaking countries to be with our family. They were basically fluent in English and really wanted to concentrate on learning to speak English even better, incorporating all of our slang along with it. I thought I might learn more Spanish by talking with them in that language, but they were not interested in speaking Spanish. Spanish speakers in that area of North Dakota were practically nonexistent, except for a few Spanish teachers in the high schools. So many desires and no way to fulfill them, I thought.

As the administration in the school system spent the summer months searching for a Spanish teacher to no avail, they considered not offering the three Spanish classes that were filled already with pre-registered students. Then somehow God got involved with the whole situation about the time for the fall semester of school to start. I received a call at my house asking me if I would come to the school and talk with them about teaching those classes. I assured them that I did not have the qualifications to do so in the area of Spanish, having not taken a Spanish class for twenty years. They insisted that I come and talk with them, so I reluctantly agreed to do so. I spoke with my husband about it, and he agreed that I should do it. I felt fear wanting to come over me, and I wanted to find a way out of this by just turning down that offer. But, God would not hear of it. I knew in my spirit that this was His doing and that I would just have to trust him.

The funny thing about all this was that the school administration was interested in me, because they knew that I had children who were well behaved and that the students in the classes that I substituted in were well behaved. They said that was half the battle of teaching, and many teachers struggled in that area. The calling of a teacher in my life included the authority and anointing to do the job well, and I knew God was with me. I prayed and depended on the Lord to help me be a mother and a substitute teacher, and now I would have to be stretched and depend on Him to help me be a contracted teacher. How would I be able to teach a language that I did not speak? I had all but given up on ever using that Spanish learned so long before. Isn't it just like God to wait until we have no ability in ourselves to do something? When God is working in our destiny, He always stretches us beyond our natural abilities. The vision for travel to Latin America had basically died in me.

Twenty years earlier the emphasis in my college Spanish courses had been on reading and writing Spanish. Very seldom did they do much with the practical aspect of speaking it fluently. Oh sure, the pronunciation skills were learned well, and there were the phrases and drills they did with the casual conversation of greeting someone and asking a few simple questions. But, I can say that I really did not acquire a speaking ability that would qualify me to be a teacher of Spanish. On top of all this, I would have to teach alongside seasoned teachers with master's degrees and many opportunities to travel to Spanish speaking countries. They knew the culture of these countries first hand and I knew nothing of it, except through books and videos. I began to compare myself to those I would have to work with and this, I learned, was not wise. There was no way I could measure up to their standards. What a dilemma I was in!

God insisted that I accept the position and told me to yield myself to his grace which was sufficient in my time of need. The Bible says this in II Cor. 12:9. I proved this to be entirely true. The other teachers in the department were more encouraging and helpful than I could ever have imagined. If it were not for their support and constant assurance that I could do this, I would have had a very difficult time struggling with my feelings of inadequacy. God had this too all arranged beforehand to see me through. We need one another, and words of encouragement can keep someone going forward into his destiny. I always remembered that I needed to do the same with those that felt inadequate around me. Encouragement is a gift from God that will inspire and develop courage and boldness in us to do what seems to be impossible.

Well, needless to say, it was a trial and a half for me the beginning months of that school year! I prayed and studied and even took a class at the college to brush up my speaking skills. The students understood my dilemma and were thankful that I had accepted the position so they could learn Spanish. I began to see things in a different light and I began thinking more about helping them than my own inadequacies. I had great classes and we accomplished so much together. God was entirely faithful to increase me in knowledge and wisdom of this language and I began to gain some confidence. In fact, I really began to enjoy teaching Spanish and knew God was up to something bigger than just these classes. It was a lot of hard work, but I realized that destiny was wrapped up in stepping out in faith in obedience to the Lord.

A funny thing also happened as I spent day after day in the school system. I began to see that my children had learned spiritual principles well and had not compromised their Christian standards to be part of the "in crowd." Many students found themselves in much trouble because there was not a firm foundation of Christian principles taught in their homes. I was a stern disciplinarian at home wanting my children to grow up serving the Lord. As I think back on those days of rearing children, maybe I was a little too unbending in some areas, but God brought us all through in spite of my shortcomings. I believed God's way was the only way. My heart was right, but I definitely needed adjustments in my character and attitudes. I learned to give more credit to my children for the way they coped with the peer pressures at school. I did not realize that the environment at school was so challenging for Christian kids and they surmounted the pressures much better than I ever would have thought. When a person only looks at things from one perspective, it seems like the world is closing in for the destruction of all godly character in today's youth. Yet, all those years of instilling in them Christian values caused a planting and grounding of those things in their hearts because of their own willingness to live a godly life. I began to praise them instead of fearing that the world system would destroy them in time.

I had to be aware of the destinies that God was preparing them for also. Sometimes I would shudder to think about them wanting to help others who could certainly pull them into a lifestyle that was not godly if I did not intervene. I realized that the callings on their lives had to be fulfilled, but I did not understand why I felt like I did. One of our children is a teacher who is especially gifted to help children who cannot learn quickly. Another is a policeman helping those in trouble with the law. The youngest is a social worker helping children in dysfunctional families. The compassion that they all had to help those, who had a hard time of it get ahead, was wonderful once I understood that was what God was doing through their callings. The perspectives we have must be God's perspectives so we do not discourage our children from their destinies. We as parents have to live without fear of our children getting in the wrong crowd, yet be wise and understanding of God's will for our children's lives and encourage and support them in their callings.

I learned many lessons from my children, and I must say that I am very grateful that we survived those growing up years as well as we did. The grace of God is a wonderful attribute with which we are blessed.

As you read on, please understand that my life as a growing Christian had lots of "bumps" in the road to my destiny. The only way that I kept on course with Jesus Christ and his plan for me was to die to my self will and yield to His. All of life is full of tests and trials to prove one's faith in the Lord and recognize what He is doing to bring one to maturity. God gives his children grace to pass the tests and rise to the next level of faith and obedience. A trust in Him develops as character is transformed and one resembles more of His image. Maturity is visible to those around us when we eventually get wisdom and experience in hearing His voice speaking truth and direction to us and then acting on it.

Would you pray this short prayer with me if you truly want to follow the Lord?

Father God, I choose to follow you with all of my heart into the paths that you have set before me. I know that I will trip and stumble along the way, but you will be there to set me back on my feet again. Help me to never give up on you or on myself as I go forward into your purposes for me. Teach me to see things from your perspective and not from mine alone. Let wisdom shape me and truth keep me. Give me an understanding heart to better relate to others. In your precious name I pray. Amen

Divine Connections

After a year of teaching and studying Spanish, I developed a greater confidence in the Lord and in my own ability to trust Him to be my provision. I realized that if I could do it, He wouldn't have to. He wanted to stretch me beyond my limits. That word limits is just so, so limiting! If I do not limit God, then there are no limits. He is totally able to do all things well.

Because God was restoring and adding an ability to me for speaking Spanish, I remembered that I would like to travel to Latin America to use this language and to help people. All the other language teachers at my school had traveled to countries that spoke the language that they taught. To experience culture firsthand was a big asset to teaching the target language. Oh, how I longed to go to Mexico or Central America to gain more understanding of Spanish. The classes went some years to other countries to get firsthand experience with the language, but selected teachers had already been assigned duties in those areas. God would have to find a way for me to go. I knew He would not fail me. If He was giving me more understanding of the language, then I knew it was for a purpose. I loved the Lord and really wanted to go on a mission trip to some country so I would be free to evangelize while I was there. God had it all planned out ahead of time and I walked right into the door of opportunity one day when I went to Canada for a church conference. There I met a person from North Dakota who told me about a mission organization out of Minnesota. She told me that they had a bus ministry to Mexico and collaborated with a Ministry in Monterrey. My heart nearly leaped out of my chest as I heard those words. Something quickened in my spirit and I just had to know more about this ministry opportunity.

I went home to my family and shared with them what that lady had told me. At first my husband had some doubts about it all. I never was away from home much in those days and there were three children to care for besides him. He certainly was not interested in going and I knew the children would be a lot of extra work without mom around. We began to pray and keep an open mind about it all. I called that ministry in Minnesota and they had room on the bus if I wanted to go. They would take a couple of trips during the summer months. The trips would start from a place in Minnesota that was about seven hours by car from where I lived in North Dakota. The cost was low because they used old, yellow school buses that had no air conditioning and ate picnic style along the way. The buses had more than one driver so they would drive straight through, stopping only for bathroom and eating breaks. The trip took about three days and was very demanding on the body because there were no showers and not much opportunity to change clothes.

I loved to "rough it" and the excitement mounted in my spirit as I thought about how much fun it would be. I knew better than to manipulate my husband into letting me go. I would have to totally depend on God to give us *both* a confirmation in our

25

spirits one way or the other. We prayed and I asked God to show me His perfect will. If He said no, then it would be no and I would have to die to my desires and prefer His. It was so hard to contain my expectations and hopes. I was learning to give everything to Him and be ready to accept disappointment if need be.

My husband was proud of me the way that I turned it over to God. I knew that he could see changes in me from the dealings of God in my life. As I learned to respond properly, my husband was drawn closer to God. My husband actually saw the signs and wonders of a wife yielding so he could have the spiritual leadership in the family. He never demanded that position God gave to him, but he had it because I finally allowed him to be the head of the family. A wife can do so much more by letting God work it out as He chooses. I began to develop a greater respect for my husband and he began to love and appreciate me more and more as he saw a godly Proverbs 31 woman emerging from time spent in relationship to Jesus Christ.

I realized that the Holy Spirit is a gentleman too and would never force His will on me. He draws us to desire to yield to the will of God, but would never demand it. The devil, on the other hand, would use coercion and manipulation to get his way like I used to do in the past. I might get my way, but I would not have peace. I began to treasure and value peace in my spirit. If there was no peace, then I could not "break down doors" to get my way. When a person does the will of God, there will be peace in his spirit.

You see, every decision we make is a choice: to die to self or to have our own way. If we get our way, then God does not get His. If He gets His way, then we have peace and He is pleased. This is the beginning of wisdom and the fear of the Lord.

God spoke to us both and we knew that this trip was another step in the right direction. The divine connections through this ministry in Minnesota proved that God was leading me forward into something greater. I literally saw the prophetic words spoken over me coming to pass.

I gave the family a little training on how to cook and keep

house while I would be away for a couple of weeks. The kids were in junior high and high school by this time so it was not a hard thing for Dennis to handle alone. The older kids were busy with summer jobs and the youngest one had her sports and her friends. We lived in an area that was close to all the places they had to go. There was an extra car so it all worked out fine. Dennis did not have to miss any work and some of our friends helped out with meals.

The day came in which I was to travel to Minnesota, and all was ready. The ride down went fine and I had a lot of time alone in the car to pray and seek the Lord. I did not really know what to expect from the trip to Mexico, but I knew I would learn a lot. At the Mexican border we all had to pray hard so that we could get all the blankets and clothing through to the people we would be ministering to. Many times the border patrol would confiscate things from mission groups for themselves or to sell. There had been incidences in the past with this bus ministry. God has a way of hiding those things that He wants us to get through to people there. We had a lot of Bibles along too and that was the most precious cargo. The Word must get into the hands of the people living in poverty conditions. There must be hope given to those people that there is a Savior who died for them and who wants to offer them salvation and eternal life in heaven.

We made it across and finished the trip by stopping at a huge church complex in Monterrey, Mexico that was used to house large groups coming to do mission work. So many emotions and so many fears were being experienced. Hardly anyone could speak a word of Spanish and what I could speak was not very fluent yet. Frustration began to set in early as the language barrier challenged us. The people there were happy to see us, of course, and would rattle away in their native tongue not realizing at first that no one had a clue what they were talking about. Even for me, the rapid talking was almost impossible to understand. I was determined to gain a better hold on it before I left and listened intently as each would speak.

The leader of the group gave us all duties to perform during the time spent there. We were all responsible for cleaning bathrooms and sleeping quarters and also preparing food, table cleanup, washing and drying dirty dishes and laundry. Everyone had to take a part. The boys were not too happy about all the kitchen work and cleaning to say the least. This too was part of mission trips. There were bunk beds and showers and indoor toilets and many, many bugs. All in all, things were very tolerable.

I was so happy to be there that it did not matter where I slept, what I ate, or what kind of bathroom facilities there were. I felt very flexible and secure in the hands of the Lord and that ministry. The Ministry there organized us into groups the following day and we went out on the streets to do evangelism to whole neighborhoods. We all had our instructions and Bibles to pass out. We were given a short course on Spanish pronunciation and papers with phrases on them. The main purpose was to lead people to a personal relationship with Jesus Christ and give them a Bible.

CHAPTER 4

Listening To God

I MET MANY WONDERFUL PEOPLE who were living in those humble shacks. Nothing is quite so rewarding as bringing people into God's Kingdom. I loved to tell them that now I knew more of my Christian family living in different places around the world. There is such a spiritual bond between God's people, and this truly is a miraculous sign of His love for his family.

There were so many experiences sharing the gospel with those Mexican people. They had such great needs in every area, but the need for a Savior was, I believe, the greatest. It was a privilege for me to be there in their country and share God's love with them. My heart was so touched and my life changed so much from those relationships.

My heart was overwhelmed with love for these Spanish people whom I did not even know. I felt God was filling me with a calling to continue to reach out to them. The Lord showed me that the only reason that some people have so much "going for them" is that they have been given an opportunity in life. When a person has an opportunity to know God, an opportunity to make money, an opportunity to meet the right people, and an opportunity for ministry, etc. he can go forward with purpose. I want to be used of God to give people who are poor and without hope the opportunity to know Jesus Christ as their personal Lord and Savior.

God had given me a desire to go to Spanish speaking countries and an ability to speak the Spanish language so that He could minister through me. I did not take lightly what God had put within me, but I did not realize how important these two desires were to my destiny.

That bus trip and opportunity for me was the beginning of so many blessings that I would not have time to relate them all here. I returned to that place in Mexico with that bus ministry about three times. I went directly with a group one year out of Wisconsin and took a small group from my church. More from around the area where I lived wanted to go and others even from Canada went. I trained them to some degree in the Spanish language and hoped that they could pronounce the words well enough to be understood. They studied all the way to Mexico in the bus and practiced and practiced to improve what they had learned. How rewarding were the results of evangelism in Spanish. Some of these people had not even done evangelism in their own country and in their own language. It was an opportunity for all those involved to continue on in mission trips in future years. Some, like me, began going every year to various mission fields in the world and being used mightily by God. That's what it is all about, isn't it? It's telling others about Jesus' love for them and giving them opportunities to share this love in ways God is leading them.

Of course, God had more than just evangelism planned for me on these trips. He was making more connections for me. Let me share with you how God worked out one of these connections. When the bus would arrive at the location where we would stay, we would all go into the dormitory or facility and find a bunk bed to place our belongings on, thus claiming that bed for our own for the duration of the time there. It happened that when we arrived, no one was in the dormitory, but there definitely were others who were staying there. I just randomly chose a bunk on the bottom and laid all my "stuff" down on it. While we were getting acclimated and cleaned up from the long trip, the others returned. It was interesting to meet the lady in the bunk right next to mine. She actually was from Finland and worked on staff with that ministry there in Monterrey. She spoke English very well and also four other languages fluently. We "hit it off" right away and knew

30

that there was something beginning to knit us together in the spirit. I told her how pleased I was that we bunked next to each other and had these wonderful times to chat.

She began to tell me how it happened that she ended up in that spot with that bunk. When she first arrived, she put her things down on the other side of that big room. There were about 100 of us staying in that room, so it was very large. She just did not feel that it was the right place and moved her things to another bunk. Many places were open because our big group had not arrived yet. This spot also did not seem like the correct one. So for the third time, she moved her things again. This was the bunk that was now next to mine. Isn't God good!

She was having some relationship problems with some people on her staff. I did not know anyone of them, of course, nor did I know anything about the situation. She had not even told me she had a problem with anything. But, God knew and He used me supernaturally with words of wisdom and knowledge to speak right into her situation. She was amazed at how the Lord provided answers to her prayers and the whole episode ended peaceably. This definitely helped our relationship with each other, and we began to write to each other during the year. I really felt a kindred spirit with her just like the one David had with Jonathon. It was a "God thing." The next year when I returned, we spent as much time together as we could around our ministry schedules. We were able to go out from the complex and eat in wonderful Mexican restaurants. This was a treat for me because all our food was prepared at the place we stayed. We ate a lot of sandwiches, beans, salads and macaroni. My bent for experiencing Mexican culture was being enlarged. I just got tastes of cultural experiences on those trips, but they equipped me better for teaching Spanish culture in my classes.

The last year that I returned to Mexico to do mission work, my friend was not there. God had given her a new assignment in Ecuador working with her church denomination out of Finland. I really missed seeing her, but we both felt that we would see each other again some day somewhere in the world. It is hard to leave it like that, but God is always faithful in his purposes for us.

I want to relate a few other experiences that happened in Mexico during those trips that will help you understand some of the lessons God taught me as I submitted my will to Him. God always "sets us up" to see His goodness and love. This particular trip, which was to be my last to Monterrey, was in a different location than the others. It brought us to a complex where there was an orphanage and a pasture for animals. There was a men's dormitory in the pasture that was vacant because the school year had ended and all had gone home. It was used as a Bible School for those going into ministry. The building was in terrible condition. It was shaped like an "L." The guys on the trip used one wing and the ladies used another. There were bars on the windows, but no glass. The curtains were see-through and did not help much to give us privacy. The guys had to stay over in their own area so as not to see things they shouldn't!

There was one fairly large room that had a pile of ground up concrete in it. There were bunks around the perimeters of the room. When I saw the bathroom, I knew we were in for trouble. The whole bathroom facility had three toilets, three sinks and three shower nozzles, but no dividers anywhere. All was out in the open and there was absolutely no privacy. In fact, there was no privacy anywhere in that building. I loved to "rough it," of course, so I began to adjust to what we had. Others, however, could not. There were women and high school girls all in one room together. God was up to something and we all had to take a good look at how good of missionaries we were. Could we understand how to give up creature comforts that we had back in the states? Was it all about us or was it about doing God's work? Such were the dealings of God that went on. Needless to say, some did not handle this situation very well.

There were so many bugs and cockroaches, cucarachas if you will. On top of this insect infestation, we were realizing that the place was full of scorpions. Now coming from North Dakota where there are no scorpions, none of us knew exactly what to do about them. I felt so confident about the insect situation because I had brought cockroach "hotels" along. The advertising said that the cockroaches walk in and never come out! No problem I thought. Would you believe not even one of those cucarachas entered that "hotel." To make matters worse, the insect spray that I had did not even phase them. Soon, the scorpions appeared and I squirted them with direct hits. Nothing happened. Now we all were getting a little uptight.

God was not through with us yet. He was making us into fearless missionaries. That night we went to bed. It was so hot and no air was entering. The women were so afraid by this time that they just covered up with their sheets completely covering their heads too. I thought they might suffocate sleeping like that. The huge cockroaches were "dive-bombing" us in the bunks. So many screams were heard as we tried to settle down and sleep. It was useless. No sleep would come.

The leader had told us to find someone as a prayer partner and each morning and night to pray with each other. This was a wonderful idea. The only catch was that we were all afraid and prayer did not seem to be helping.

As I laid in my bunk praying furiously for God to protect me against the cockroaches and against the scorpions and against whatever dangers were lurking outside my window, I heard a still, small voice inside my spirit say that a spirit of fear was the problem. The enemy was not the bugs and scorpions and dangers, but the enemy was FEAR. When I realized that God had spoken this and that I had authority over fear, I rebuked it in the name of Jesus and in an instant I was free. I praised the Lord and trusted my life into the hands of the one who would protect me. I slept like a baby that night.

Let me continue to share what fears we further had to overcome in that place in Mexico. I described our bathroom facility earlier. There was no privacy as I said. One of the ladies who was very overweight and very self-conscious of her body would not take a shower when we all were present. Consequently, she did not go out on the streets evangelizing with us. She also was afraid that someone would come in and steal our possessions and clothes while we were away doing ministry. I later found out that she had brought a child's inflatable swimming pool along, and she used that to take a bath in while we were out. No one was around and she was secure to bathe properly and also protect all of our belongings. I felt badly for her because she had come all that way to minister in evangelism, and she was not participating in any of it.

One evening while some of us were taking showers in that bathroom, one lady happened to look up at the small window high on the wall. She let out a terrible scream, grabbed her towel, and ran out. We all looked up and saw a man watching us take showers through that window. Someone yelled to the men on the other wing of the building telling them what happened. Some of them chased this man but could not catch him. He had made himself a platform of wooden boxes in the back to peep in the window at us. We felt so violated, and now fear really began to grow. How long had this gone on unnoticed, we wondered? What more would we have to deal with in that place?

I shared what God showed me about the spirit of fear and how I dealt with it. The ladies realized that this was the problem they were having too. There were just too many things that were causing us to be afraid. The enemy truly was FEAR. We prayed together, and God set us all free from fear. Then we began to enjoy the purpose we were there for. My prayer partner happened to be this heavy set lady who bathed in the swimming pool. She was so shy and reserved having to deal with all these conditions and her inhibitions and fears. When we broke that spirit of fear, she turned into the most fun person of the whole group. She had a sense of humor that kept us laughing day and night. We could hardly believe it was the same lady. When God took away her fear, he took away her fear of everything. That spirit of fear is so prevalent in so many people. Without a Word of Knowledge through the Holy Spirit, a person can stay bound with fear her whole life. God is so good to always meet our every need, and He is a very present help in the time of trouble says His Word.

I found out that the men were dealing with these same fears also, and we all understood that through these trials, we had become stronger. God is so faithful to His Word.

It is hard to have a calm spirit when there is fear present. That is why Jesus must be our peace in the midst of trials. When we yield to His peace, then we will hear His voice showing us what to do. Reaction must give way to faith in God, and He will make a way for us.

Would you like to pray with me to give your fears to God and see Him set you free so you can be who He created you to be?

Heavenly Father, I acknowledge that I do have fears, and I have not trusted you like I should. Forgive me Lord, for doubting your ability to protect me. Today, I take authority over my fears and I declare in the name of Jesus that fear has to leave. Spirit of fear, you cannot overpower me. I chose to stand on your Word, Lord, and take dominion over my thoughts. I believe in my heart that You are Lord, and all things are under my feet. Thank you for the faith you have given me to know that you are in control of all situations. Please increase my understanding, Lord, of how powerful you are. In your holy name, Amen.

Many souls were won to the Kingdom of God that week and Satan did not stop what God ordained for such a time as this. So many families were given Bibles and invited to a church where they could be taught the Word of God and find fellowship among other believers. If we will keep focused on what He is doing, we will see victory in every situation. God truly does go before us and prepares the way.

I made four trips to Mexico doing evangelism and also building houses out of concrete. A missionary must be a "jack of all trades" because one never knows what will be required to show God's love and spread His Word. The poverty was so over-whelming and no one could ever minister there and remain the same in his heart. My love grew and grew as God filled it with these Mexican people who needed a Savior. I knew that God was just beginning to lead me in His paths of faith and love. Even when I was home in North Dakota my heart cried with them in their need both spiritual and financial. What destiny lies ahead for them I thought? How will they ever find fulfillment in God's Kingdom? Who will give them more opportunities? I thought, so many people and so little time. The harvest truly is ready and there is great need of workers to bring it in.

One last example of how God had prepared the hearts of the people to receive His Word will suffice to demonstrate how important it is to be obedient to the voice of His Spirit. A couple of us were just finishing up delivering our New Testaments and sharing the love of Jesus. I had one Bible left in my backpack and the time had almost arrived to return and join the rest of the group. My friend and I were quite far up on a mountain and had a long ways to walk back. There were a few more humble houses up the mountain yet to reach, but we only had one Bible left. What should we do? We were thinking of going back to the bus. One Bible could be saved for the next day's outreach possibly. I prayed, Lord show me what to do with this last Bible. God immediately gave me an answer. I felt to walk up a very small path off to the right of where we were. My friend agreed and off we went. We walked several yards up and finally saw a small house. When the lady of the house saw us approaching, she ran out to meet us. She was very excited and happy to see us. We had not encountered anyone doing this before on our outreaches there. Her house seemed to be all by itself on this little path. Could it be a divine encounter of the Lord, I wondered? This little lady told us that she had been praying for several days for the Lord to show her somehow that He was real and loved her. She had asked Him to send someone with a Bible if He truly cared about her.

We were an answer to that prayer and God knew all along that this day would come and that we would go. The fear of the Lord came into me right there as I thought about what if we would not have gone. We all praised God and prayed and kissed each other. God had done a wonderful work of faith and grace in all of our hearts that day. We literally floated down the mountain to return to the bus. What a blessing to be the servant of the Lord and be obedient to the heavenly calling.

Many others had similar incidents happening to them also. No one can tell me that God does not hear our prayers and move his people into position for harvest. My trust in God began to build as I saw His miraculous love for His people. Praise be to the Lord!

Getting Excited

Doors were beginning to open for me as I continued to teach Spanish part time in the public school system. I was beginning to travel more with my husband as our children became older and more self- sufficient. I taught some adult education Spanish classes and enjoyed substituting in many various classes. My love for teaching Spanish was growing and God's grace was helping me improve my fluency. It would have been nice to be very fluent very fast, but God assured me it would come as I kept using it. I had a desire to have a very good command of this language so that I could minister well in it. Deep down in my spirit I knew that I would be doing ministry in other countries where Spanish was spoken.

We accepted an exchange teacher from the country of Costa Rica. This lovely lady was a joy to have around. She was an English as a Second Language (ESL) teacher in her country and came to see how our ESL classes were taught so she could learn and teach new techniques to her pupils. She arrived in the winter and had never experienced the below zero temperatures that we had in North Dakota. She suffered those cold months while she was there. She said there were no words in her vocabulary to explain that kind of cold. The closest she could come to explaining that cold was to tell them to sit inside a freezer full of ice. We laughed as we shared stories of our individual cultures. It was a good learning experience for me as I continued to gather knowledge of people in Latin America. The next year I was able to travel to Costa Rica to visit her and a mutual acquaintance that we had there. I found the accent harder to understand in Costa

Rica than in Mexico. This too was a new challenge for me with the language. I listened carefully and learned much in my time spent there.

Our connections to several churches in Canada opened doors for more mission trips, but this time to Guatemala. This country was also in Central America and was fairly unsettled at this time. It had somewhat of a military government and the presence of armed guards all around was a bit unnerving. I was not used to anything like this.

We traveled to Guatemala by plane which I was thankful for. It would have taken at least two weeks by bus from North Dakota. The group was small and was made up of a pastor, a missionary, church leaders and one female the age of my daughter. There were seven of us in all. Everyone was going on this trip for the first time except the missionary. He was fluent in Spanish and had helped churches there to get stronger and have tools to better minister in the area. This country was very poor and was not unlike Mexico in certain respects. The language spoken there was easier for me to understand. I did not have any interpreter but had to be one for the others who knew no Spanish. I again was challenged with learning vocabulary that I did not learn in college. As we all worked together building houses, wells, outhouses, and kilns for baking bread, the language became easier with time. The people were so friendly and appreciative of our help. We were privileged to eat tortillas, beans and rice with them. They ate this every day. Once in a while there would be chicken and/or fish. The fruit from various trees provided us with many new and wonderful tastes.

At that time in my life I loved to minister to little children. We were always surrounded by them, and they could understand me fairly well. My friend helped me and we were so blessed to see them understanding Bible verses and asking Jesus to be their Lord. We brought little bracelets and craft items for them to make. This was something that they had never had where they lived. The poverty was very severe here. The children only needed about five dollars in our money to go to school. They had to buy materials and a notebook. About one half of the children could not afford to go to school even though the school was situated right across the road. This broke my heart to see. When I returned home to North Dakota, I was able to speak about my trip to various churches in the community. Some of them began to make book bags and fill them will school supplies. The following year when I returned, these children were furnished with what they needed to go to school.

I had the calling to be a teacher of Spanish, but now I was using that Spanish to teach those children how to minister unto the Lord. We had so much fun learning together. They taught me their language and I taught them the Bible and Sunday School songs. As I returned each year for four years, I brought supplies for their Sunday Schools that they got started. There were flannelgraphs and wonderful books with stories and puppets. Oh, how they loved the puppets. These were such a great teaching tool for them and held them enrapt for long periods of time sitting on the ground in the hot, humid climate. I pray that God will introduce me to those children again when I get to heaven. I pray that more opportunities come for them to become teachers also.

I was acquiring a pretty good knowledge of how to build a house made of cement blocks. I worked right along with the men, digging out the foundation with a shovel. The ground was so hard that we would have to carry pail after pail of water from the well to wet the ground so that we could dig in it. We dug out the holes for the outhouses this way too. It was hard ground and hard work. I thought about the soil of my heart and hoped that Jesus did not have this much trouble digging up my soil. It was so special to see the well. It was exactly like the kind that you would see in the Jack and Jill nursery rhyme. I realized that the well was used for so many purposes. These people in this area had no training on hygiene or sanitation. The wells were very contaminated and they suffered from drinking water without boiling it. Most everyone in the village went without shoes and they picked up parasites and hookworms very easily because the animals were free to roam where they wanted to eat the rinds of fruit that was discarded.

When the children fell and hurt themselves playing, dirt would get in the open wounds. They did not know to wash out the wound to cleanse it and keep out infection. Our team taught them the simple rules of digging wells away from out houses, slanting the soil away from the base of the well, keeping the pail tied to the rope and not letting it touch the ground and then be thrown back into the well. We chlorined the well and made it pure again. I showed the children how to immediately cleanse their wounds and also wash their hands before eating. This was all foreign to them. One child I saw lost his sight in one eye because he rubbed his eye with dirty hands and got an infection in it that was not treated. This is so sad and needless. If only more opportunities were there for them to be taught. A person must look for every opportunity and meet it in the short stay with the people. Every little teaching is like a treasure to them, because it can actually save their lives or at least give them longer lives. The average life span is less than 50 years there. I pray progress and more help will give them a better life.

In one of the locations where we ministered, the missionary taught the pastors in one area, another lady and I taught the children in another area a few feet away from the pastors, another small group of ladies was learning how to make bracelets close by, a house was being build for the pastor not far from the other groups and in the little church, a nurse was seeing patients and treating them using the medicine that we had brought down. All this went on under the palms trees since there was not a place large enough to house us all. It was a joy to see so much being accomplished at one time in one day. We spent usually a week or so in each village we visited.

The women from the village would walk a mile to a creek to wash the basket full of clothes they carried on top of their heads. It was a heavy load on the way back because it was wet. The ladies would also all have a baby nestled in a shawl tied around their neck and resting on their back. They worked very hard and did not stand even five feet tall; a small people they were. The clothes were laid to dry over grass and tree branches when they returned back to their houses. Their houses were made of bamboo poles, split and tied together with vines. The floor was dirt and the roof was made of woven palm branches. The house was one room that held a bench or two and maybe a mat was on the floor. If they could afford a hammock, there may be one of those hanging along one wall. The houses were round in shape usually. The family slept on woven mats at night. The insects were very bad and there was no escape from them. They, of course, had no repellent. When it got dark, there was not any light except the moon. There was no electricity to many of the villages. Our group was able to help to get a generator and a cord with a light bulb or two on it for meetings under the trees at night. The area was not a dense jungle, but nevertheless, it was full of trees and undergrowth.

We had wonderful services with songs and preaching. Any outside guests always were welcome and there was much rejoicing because the Lord was doing a good work among them. Surrounding churches would join us at times and all provided music and special songs from their culture. Even the prophetic song flowed as the anointing increased and the Holy Spirit was released. I will always carry the memory of those times in my heart.

CHAPTER 5

Surprises

I LOVED TO TEACH THE CHILDREN in the streets. I would start out with a few, and as they accepted Jesus into their hearts, they had a desire to tell others. I brought craft supplies along for 200 children and every morning and afternoon we had classes. My goal was to train them to be little evangelists to the community. The crafts would always have an implication towards salvation. The children used bracelets most of the time to share with others their own age what the different colored beads represented. They would help them understand how sin was in their lives and how the cleansing power of Jesus' blood gave them new life and growth in the knowledge of Him through studying His Word. As the week progressed, the numbers grew until we fully had 200 children being taught at one time. They did the work of an evangelist and invited all those children to the classes I was teaching. I did not have much help because those that came from Canada did not speak Spanish. They would help me with the crafts and to keep things in order. These were children who spent most of their time running in the streets finding whatever to do. They were used to fist fighting and holding their own to survive. It was a real challenge for me to speak Spanish fluently, so they could understand and also to keep the activities moving. I always involved them in the teaching so that they would learn how to teach the other children who did not know Jesus. They learned with diligence many Bible verses. I would print a word or two of the Bible verse on a laminated piece of construction paper. They would learn the verse by repeating it over a few times, and then, I would pick certain ones each day to hold a word and the others had to stand them in the right order to make the verse read correctly. They had a lot of fun learning scripture this way. At the end of the week, many could recite those verses with no help from me. I pray that they will always stay in their hearts. All my materials were left for the church to use in Sunday School classes in days ahead.

It was such a joy to see the enthusiasm and hunger in the children to learn who Jesus is. What a privilege to teach the little ones about the Kingdom of God that was come to them in that humble place. Each year they looked for the bus to come bringing the teacher. Each year the number of children grew. The parents even wanted to learn as the children did. God was faithful.

Teaching the children would cover the morning and early afternoon of each day. After I had lunch together with the other members of the team, I would visit the different outreaches that were going on. Many were building a house for the pastor and his family out of concrete. There was no interpreter to help with the instructions until I arrived. It was amazing how much they could do by watching. Our contractors taught the nationals how to do it by demonstrating and then allowing them to learn. This was a trade learned that would allow them to have a better job and earn more money. An average job paid less than a dollar a day. They were used to hard work and were excited to learn new things. Some were distributing clothing that we had brought along. It had to be sorted according to who would wear it. It was a real blessing to see them wear those things that we had brought. The missionary in charge would do leadership classes to train the national pastors so they would grow in the knowledge of the truth.

These churches that we worked with in the cities were very legalistic and formal. The women would sit on one side and the men on the other. Even husbands and wives did not sit together. We had to do likewise when we attended services with them. The religion and culture was very different from ours, but we were there to show them the freedom of the Holy Spirit and release the spiritual gifts that lie within them. This could be done within the context of the services, and they were realizing that church could be exciting and fun. The children were most enthusiastic, and little by little they were given opportunities to participate too. I heard little boys of 8 years of age pray and share their faith with such boldness and anointing that I knew the leaders in the next generation would be powerful and see God move mightily in that place. If they would just be given opportunities for growth, God would be faithful to develop their potential.

Each night we would go to a different church, some in the city and some in the country. Such humble buildings and so lacking of comforts, but filled with the glory of God. God moved in the prophetic word to encourage and strengthen those churches. God knew exactly what situations existed and moved through man to communicate how He was building his church there. It was divine revelation from God because no man knew anything about what was happening in these churches. God has given spiritual gifts to his church as it says in I Corinthians. These gifts are for edification, comfort and exhortation so that there would be the character of Christ visible in their lives. It must "look like Jesus" if it is to be His body of believers. It was fun to watch them grow in the knowledge of Him as we returned year after year to the same places.

We had a lot of unusual things happen as we worshiped, worked, and ate together. One trip, when we were eating under the trees at a wooden picnic table, was just such a time. We had stopped at a little store en route to the village. It had a glass case filled with rolls, and our leader bought two sacks of rolls. That year there was a small delegation from Canada and myself from North Dakota. We were enjoying the fresh fruit and the food prepared for us including the rolls we had purchased. I was talking and paying no attention to the roll I was enjoying. When I finished eating it, the man next to me told me to take another roll and open it up. As I did so, I saw that it was full of small, live ants. I asked him if the other one was too? He said it was, and I realized that I had eaten many live ants without knowing it. Now what was I going to do? I was a woman, and probably should have screamed at this point, thinking about eating live ants. The adventurer rose up in me, and I tried to be very brave. One of the men was capturing it all on video by this time. The group had seen me eating that roll with the ants and just wanted to see what I would do as they had a little fun with it all. I could not believe I was so intent on talking that I did not even look to see what I was eating! I never worried about such things anyway. My stomach was not bothered by anything I had ever eaten on those trips. With another roll in my hand with more live ants on it, I proceeded to knowingly eat that one too. They could not believe I did it, and frankly, I could not believe either what I had done. We laughed so hard, and they will always have on video what happened. The first chance I got, I asked one of the natives there what would happen if someone ate live ants. She said that they would bite me. I did not feel anything biting me inside, so I decided that I would live! It tickles me each time I think about it though.

Because I could speak Spanish, I had many opportunities to sit on a dirt floor in one of their huts and visit with the women. One lady shared her experiences of childbirth with me. There were no doctors there and the women had their babies without medical help. They knew what must be done and the culture was such as this. When there was a complication, "What did you do?" I asked. I thought about breach births and other things that might go wrong. That lady pulled up her blouse and showed me just what did happen to her. The baby would not come and trauma was setting in. Another heated a machete in the fire and somehow an incision was made in her abdomen with that machete and the baby delivered. The scars of that procedure and the infection that still was present sent chills up my spine. How that woman suffered to deliver that baby. I could not even imagine living life day after day with such primitive tools for survival. I prayed a prayer of healing for her and many others who had suffered because of no medical attention. They must know the God who heals and restores in a fuller way. They relied on their God for all their needs because there were no facilities available for emergencies.

There were combined groups of Canadians from different providences and myself from North Dakota on one of the trips.

This particular time, it was a group of doctors and nurses as well as others from some churches in British Columbia. We all stayed in a facility that was very nice and used to house missionaries. Other times we had stayed in a small motel complex that was close to where we worked. Our hotel cost three dollars a night and provided a bed, toilet, and shower. It was all we needed.

We left the large facility traveling on a school bus and headed down the highway to a small village. On the way, we came upon a bridge that had been destroyed by a bomb that morning. Many people were standing on the bridge as well as some military personnel and the media. We asked what was happening and were told that terrorist guerrillas had done it, and that they were rising up again to take control of the country. This country had to deal with these situations frequently and the army was very much a presence in all of that area.

I thought that this was a real tragedy and a great hardship for these people who lived in fear of their lives every day. There had been boards laid on the bridge that was resting on one bank of the river. It had not completely collapsed into the water. I saw trucks unloading their cargo each on their particular sides and exchanging it so that they could receive their money for the work that day. It amazed me how they always knew how to remedy the situation in which they were. They were pushing appliances up the planks and even a small pickup was being helped across. As we watched with interest and a little apprehension, we suddenly heard shots being fired from rifles. We were under attack and nowhere to go. Everyone immediately fell to the ground and began to crawl out of the area. Our bus was a few yards away, and all of us made it back safely. As far as I know, no one that was there was shot. The army that was by the bridge returned fire driving the guerrillas back into the jungle. Our bus had to return to the city and wait until the next day to continue with the outreach. We had to go the long way around on the other side of the mountain. No one was allowed to travel on the roads at night because of the terrorist situation. The next day, I read about it in the papers and realized that I had taken the same picture of the bridge that the

47

media had in the paper. It was a narrow escape, but God had made a way for us. We praised the Lord that none were hurt, and we spent the time praying back at the facility where we stayed. Later on that year, I returned to that same area to work and saw by that bridge, a large semi completely burned out by terrorist bombs. The bridge was guarded day and night now by the army so that the highway would be safe. I knew that God had protected us and we were grateful to be alive. I felt so sorry for the people who lived in that country in the midst of constant fear of attack. Many of them were killed. The terrorists would find a farm and demand that the owners take care of them and hide them from the army. If the peasants agreed, it was hardship for the family. If they did not, it was certain death. Many times there was death in whatever decision was made because the army would severely punish all who cooperated with the terrorists even if it was against their will.

We did many wonderful medical clinics for the people treating many ailments and diseases. The people came for free medical attention that they so desperately needed and left with salvation in their hearts and medicine and a new set of clothes. We blessed them as much as we could in that short time. They understood that there was a God who loved them and sent his love in human bodies. Some of the pregnant women were so grateful to the doctors and missionaries that they named their babies after the doctor that had treated them. It was a humbling experience to see the work of the Kingdom reach the lost and hurting. God will use the one who is willing to go and willing to be used. There are so many opportunities to reach the harvest, but the laborers are few. God is waiting for you, dear reader, to step into his plan for your life. Will you find a place to give to those who need to receive a touch from the Lord?

Would you pray with me concerning this step of faith to reach the lost and hurting in the world?

Lord Jesus, forgive me for not having eyes to see the great harvest that is ripe. Open my eyes, Lord to see what you see. Give me an opportunity and I will take hold of it and go where you direct me and do what you want me to do. Only by your grace

can I walk into what you have ordained for me to do. I am will-
ing, Lord, here am I send me. Send me to my neighbor, send me
to my friends. I will do your will and lift up your name. Let my
light shine for you and bring hope to those that are in need.
Amen and amen.

One night as I was lying on my bed there in Guatemala, I began to sob and sob. My heart was breaking for the condition of the hearts of the people and also the conditions they had to live in. I felt so inadequate and small. What could I do with such a great need? I prayed for God to show me how I could even make a difference in all these lives. How could I reach them I prayed. God spoke to me so clearly that night. He said you will reach them one by one! Oh, how my soul was set free. I rejoiced that I was counted worthy to serve Him and his people in that part of the world. I would win them one by one. I would pray and go and share the love of God. The opportunities would be arranged by the Lord, but the obedience would come from me. He would make a way.

God gave me a song from that experience. I will share it with you. It goes like this:

"Prepare me oh Lord for the task I must do. Give me more love
for the world and for you. Open my eyes Lord to see what you
see. Unlock the doors Lord, I'm here, send me. You've put in my
hands the sword and the shield. Your spirit has shown me the
white of the fields. You showed me your heart, Lord, so that I
might know, what caused you from heaven for the earth to go. I
see them, oh Jesus, I see what you see. They're needy and help-
less, lost and deceived. I'm ready to go now to show them the
way. I've seen your heart Lord, I'll reach them today."

I made those four trips to Guatemala and then the Lord did a new thing in my life. He was beginning to bring greater responsibility and anointing for His work to be done.

CHAPTER 6

Ecuador

O NE YEAR WHEN I WAS STILL GOING TO WORK in Guatemala for a couple weeks at a time, I received a letter from my friend from Finland whom I had met in Mexico. She asked me to come and help her in Ecuador where she was working at that time. Isn't it interesting how we meet people along the way in our journey to our destiny? I prayed about the invitation to help, but I did not have a release in my spirit to do so. I surely wanted to go and help, but I knew that I must have permission from the Holy Spirit to do so or I would not go. Wisdom had taught me over the years that I did not want to be out of the Father's will no matter how badly I wanted to do something. I told her that it was not to be, but I would continue to pray for God's timing. Each year she would ask if I could come and help, but it wasn't until 1993 that God opened the way for me to go. I always asked Him for many confirmations from different sources to assure me that it actually was the right timing to go. Many prophetic words were spoken to me during that time as confirmation of right timing and also there were other things that happened to tell me that now was the time.

I traveled to Ecuador alone and she met at the airport. It was such a joy to see her again. We both knew God had joined us together in ministry to Latin people. It seemed God always had very specific purposes for me when He sent me into a certain area and I was to find out exactly why I was there at that time.

The first night I arrived after a long day of flying was interrupted by a phone call about 3:00 A.M. We were both sleeping soundly in our respective rooms and felt that a call at that hour was an emergency situation at the other end. My friend answered the phone and I got up to see if I could help. When she was finished talking, she said that a friend of hers from the church was in the jungle a distance away and was in serious trouble with his health. He had a friend there that had informed us saying that this man was in a coma and his heart was palpitating and all was critical. I knew by the Spirit what God was showing me about this situation. It was a spirit of death that was upon him and he would surely die if action was not taken. I prayed a prayer in Jesus' name rebuking that spirit of death upon him. I asked God to set him totally free from it and completely heal him. I also said, in faith, that this man would be at her door in two days and be perfectly fine. I was amazed at my boldness and confidence in the matter. But, I knew it was God showing me these things. There was a peace in our spirits and we knew the prayer was answered. We went back to bed and slept peaceably throughout the night. I pondered the incident in my heart and then basically forgot about it.

Two days later early in the morning about 6:00, there was a knock on the door. I did not know who it was when I answered it. My friend was upstairs getting ready for the day and I told her she had company. This person seemed to have been at the house before and was comfortable there. As we walked upstairs, my friend saw him and was very surprised. She said that this is the man we prayed for two nights ago. I could hardly believe what I was hearing. God was faithful to heal him and bring him to the door two days later. We rejoiced in the miracle and knew that God was doing a wonderful work of restoration in our faith.

The time spent in Ecuador was full of ministry to many people. God is never late with what He wants to do. It is so incredible to see how He works things out even within minutes of someone possibly dying. He brought a Minnesota farm girl all the way to Ecuador at that precise moment to hear from God and pray the right prayer, to have a Word of Knowledge about someone she had never seen, and keep death away. God surely was up to something. As it turned out, the man was in a terrible mess in his

52

marriage and was running away from a situation which he could not handle.

The spirit of death comes upon us if we are careless and open a door with our desires. It is a serious thing to say, "I wish I could die" with a strong desire to do so. The enemy will create a way for us to escape and it will be to our death. He comes to kill and destroy life while Jesus comes to give us life more abundantly. Jesus makes a way for us to escape our trials also, but His way is to do it His way! He gives us solutions and wisdom and knowledge from on high. He is the Way to life!

It is a beautiful thing to see people go on to fulfill their destinies. He has a special purpose for each one of us and will use whatever means He must, to get us to our final destination. I always desire fulfillment for myself and for others who long to be all that God called them to be in complete obedience to all God asks. There are many tests and trials along the path, but God is always faithful if we surrender to His will. Even when we do not know what we are doing, God will take us into what He wants us to be if we let Him.

The last night of my stay with my friend, was a night of a power outage in the whole city, even in most of the country. There was rationing of electrical power and water in those days. Many friends I had made in the church and community gathered at the place where I was staying and we were all in the dark except for candlelight. They had come to say goodbye. It was so hard to leave them all, but I knew it was what I had to do. We prayed, sang songs with a guitar, ministered to one another and fellowshipped. God gave me a Word for the young man who came back from a near death experience. I laid my hands on him and confirmed to him the calling of a pastor. He was totally absorbed in the anointing that was on him. It was a powerful demonstration of the will of God coming to pass. He knew that this call on his life was what God wanted him to do.

Another year when I returned to the same area, I was told that he was studying for the ministry in another city. He has become a pastor as God ordained and his marriage was restored. What the enemy meant for evil, God meant for good!

Other trips to Ecuador opened up many doors of ministry to me. God used me several times to preach and teach, especially to the women. To see them set free was such a joy to me. There were so many tragic family situations that God had to minister into. His supernatural understanding and wisdom was such a blessing since I had no way to know how to counsel unless He intervened. He never let me down and when truth was spoken, people were free. There were so many lies and deceptions that came from the enemy of their soul. The truth of God's Word applied in each situation set the captives free from bondage. Their countenances changed as they learned to see things from God's perspective and not theirs. I taught them how to stay focused on God and His plan for them. He would show them the way to walk and lead them into His truth and purposes.

Every morning when I got up I spent time reading my Bible. They kept me very busy ministering while I was in Ecuador. That particular morning I was reading in the book of Daniel about how he interpreted dreams under the anointing and revelation of God. I prayed that God would also give me this ability and use me in high places. It was not fifteen minutes later, that the telephone rang. It was the president of the 700 Club in Quito, Ecuador. Quito was the capital city and I was in a town about a half hour away. The president had heard from one of her staff that had ministered with me that signs and wonders were happening in my ministry. She said that this person on her staff would pick me up in a couple of hours and bring me to the 700 Club to meet her. I did not have a clue what that was all about, nor what I would be asked to do. I was thrilled to say the least that God was doing something special. My goal is just to set people free so that they can be what God wants them to be. He will put the pieces together and get the place and timing perfect according to His plan.

I arrived at the 700 Club, which was in a tall building in the main center of Quito. It was not a separate building, but several rooms on an upper floor. There was no TV program associated with this particular Club. The president greeted me and immediately asked me to pray for her. What I prayed was very prophetic and to the point and she was so thrilled. She said no one could have known those things except God. Then she asked me to sit down in front of her desk. As she was being seated also, she began to relate three dreams that she had had. She told them to me all the while speaking in Spanish, and I was listening with my spirit. I did not understand every word with my mind, but my spirit knew exactly what these dreams were all about. God revealed them to me as she talked. When she finished, I told her what each dream meant, how they were connected to one another, what she was holding in her hand in the dream and where to find confirmation of it all in the Bible. This was astounding to her and also to me. God is so incredibly supernatural and spontaneous to reveal all this. I knew then that reading in the book of Daniel in the morning and praying for that anointing was not a coincidence. God had that all planned for that place at that time, and I was privileged to be the instrument He used to do it. Now, that builds a person's faith in God's faithfulness!

This wonderful Christian lady then said that I was an angel sent from God. I tried to take that in, but I just knew that there was no way I could have known all that would transpire. She then invited me to go with her downtown. She had many friends in high places that were believers. She had told them her dreams and no one could interpret them. When she introduced me, she introduced me as an angel of God and shared that I had given the correct interpretation through revelation from God. We went to see several business owners, and then, we went by taxi to a penthouse on the other side of the big city of Quito. There lived a German family. The wife had serious arthritis and was getting very crippled. She was in a lot of pain. There were a couple of sons also and a husband who were present. The lady was very ill and in bed when we arrived. We went into her bedroom and I waited on the Lord to show me what to do. We basically visited and met her family. I prayed with one of her sons who was in the university and home for the lunch hour. He received the anointing that flowed through my hands and I knew that God released him from some apprehensions and tensions he possessed. The little gal that helped this family, prepared a nice lunch for us, and we conversed in Spanish about Germany and politics in the United States. I am from a German background, and so I got along just fine with them all. I even remembered a few German phrases I had picked up along the way.

When we finished eating, we went to the living room and the lady who was crippled asked me to pray for her. She started to laugh as joy filled her heart. She laughed and laughed and so did the rest of us. She told me she had never laughed when someone had prayed for her before, but instead had wept. I knew God was setting her free from her frustrations and fears. She asked me to pray for her healing and as I laid hands on her, she began to straighten out her fingers and limbs and got up and began to move about freely. God had done a miracle and her family was there to see it! We thanked God and rejoiced in His faithfulness to his people.

Time was passing fast, and we needed to return to the 700 Club for a meeting. The oldest son gave us a ride in his car, and we were there in no time. Many people were waiting for us to arrive, and there was great expectation in the air. I was asked to share a teaching from God's Word and minister to the needs of the people. Again God was so faithful to release people from their captivities, whether spiritual, emotional or physical. What a blessing it is to see people set free and built up with the Word of God.

I had to leave them there and go back to the town I was staying in to minister in the church that night. They asked me to come back when I could and minister again. They were so precious and hungry for the things of God. I did get back there another year when I was visiting Ecuador. There is a bond in the spirit with the president of that Club and also with the people who were there. I always wished I had more time to spend in these places, but God has not allowed that to be so. The family of God has something special that those who do not know the Lord personally cannot understand. It does not matter where you are in the world, or what language is spoken, there is a family relationship in the spirit. It is a supernatural knitting together in faith and love. No words can really explain the things of the spirit, but there is a knowing that they are the Lord's doing.

There were four trips to Ecuador in the 90's and into the year 2000. There was so much adventure and ministry. We sometimes had to walk across very deep ravines to get to people on the other side. There would be only a plank of wood across the chasm, and we would have to have good balance to keep from falling off. The hunger of the people kept us going to visit their villages. So many humble places that God chose to minister to, were almost impossible to reach. I knew that God was taking me to those "far corners of the world." I did not know exactly where they were, but I prayed to go to those places. I had a supernatural ability not to be affected by whatever conditions, food or water were present. I could do without any comforts and still be full of joy. I know that God made me that way, or else I could not do what I was doing. Someone must go to those out of the way places. I have found that many times, the most miraculous things happen in these places. God is so faithful to me, and He gives me so much confirmation that this type of ministry really is in my heart. It is not a hard thing for me because of the anointing. Now, I understand better what some of the disciples went through and survived. It was because of the anointing that was present in them. That anointing is a special grace that divinely enables a person to go through impossible experiences.

One relationship led to another in Ecuador and soon I had many wonderful friends there. Each place I visited had its own set of blessings and ministry to the people. Some of the areas were so impoverished that the children and parents sifted through the garbage thrown in the street for anything that they could find to eat. The need was so great and I felt so small to help. The Lord sees all those people so hungry in the natural and sends someone to feed them in the spiritual. Just bringing the good news of the gospel can change their focus and they can understand that God does care for them. Helping them to receive the Holy Spirit per-

57

sonally into their lives and connecting them with a church in the area was a big help. The churches, though poor also, could give them help and a support group for fellowship and teaching. As we help the churches financially, they in turn will have enough to help feed the hungry and clothe the naked. I went into homes that were not at all fit for life or adapted for colder evenings in the winter. Small babies had to fight for their lives to stay alive and many died. Some even died that I had held and prayed for because they could not endure the conditions and infestations of insects and germs. It is a sad thing and happens all over the world every day. We have to bring them hope of a better life and give them an inner joy and peace even in the midst of the suffering. Only Jesus Himself can do this as lives are surrendered to Him and they begin to live according to His Word. The churches have a very big responsibility to take care of the poor as the Bible says. These are all God's creation and need to be given opportunities to have a better life and lifestyle. It is too big for one, but together we can reach the world and bring the light of the gospel to them and be a blessing.

Many times in Ecuador, the farmers and others living in rural areas rose up to protest the lack of sufficient support for the products they sold. Prices were very low and it was almost impossible to provide for a family. One way they would protest is to pull big mounds of dirt and debris onto the highways thus blocking them to traffic. Many such mounds could be found within a few miles of each other. The ones who did these things sometimes would even pile them with tree branches and light them on fire so no one could remove them for a long time. Sometimes they would be present and prevent anyone from removing them all the while shouting out their opinions of the government. The government had to always send troops from the army to clear them away and deal with the problem. We ran across many of these blockades and even were looked on with disdain because they thought we were tourists who did not understand their dilemmas in that country. It was such a great help to speak Spanish because then they relaxed and thought maybe we lived there too. The soldiers all carried rifles with them even when they were working to clear the road. It was a little unnerving, to say the least, under tensions that were high. This still goes on today and is an effective way for them to voice their opinion only at the cost of others' inconvenience, which is the purpose. The governments have had problems over many years and have a very hard time to deal with the issues at hand because of lack of funds and corruption. Many governments change hands frequently because of overthrows to oust a leader who is not doing a good job or because militants want to take control and run the country. Much terrorism is still involved in mountainous, jungle-like areas and it is not entirely safe to travel on the highways especially at night. There are many bandits who rob and even kidnap and kill at times. It makes it hard for even the tourists to travel to beautiful places and partake of the wonderful culture there. Without tourist trade in some areas, the economy greatly suffers. People do not want to travel where it is not totally safe.

I had some friends who were missionaries in a town in the mountains close to the Colombian border. They were doctors from Finland and traveled to Quito regularly for ministry purposes. They had adopted a little boy from the country and were going to return to Finland for Christmas. Against their better judgment, they traveled by night in their car loaded with suitcases and gifts from Ecuador. Also the adoption papers for their son were with them in the car. In a place in the mountains where there was a curve and a grade to climb, robbers jumped out in front of the car holding guns pointed at the windshield. They had to stop, of course, and were forced out of the car. The robbers stole the car with all of their belongings and left them standing on the side of the road in the black of night. They lost everything. How tragic these situations are to deal with. Reports of such things keep others from wanting to travel to these precarious places. In all the times that I traveled on that highway, God took very good care of us as we prayed and trusted our lives into His hands.

There were many checkpoints along the road just for that reason, to keep a record of who had been traveling on the highway. These check points were a real headache too because they would take our passports and not give them back for a long time. The detainment was for the purpose to make us give them money to let us go sooner. Their salaries for these types of jobs were very low and they had to get extra money in this way without really doing something illegal. It was common knowledge that it occurs and we waited a long time, but did not have to pay anything. Had it taken a really long time, we might have had to do something to help the situation be remedied. The culture of a country should be studied a little bit before traveling or otherwise a person could get very frustrated at all the things that cause delays. We are such an impatient people and money is worth less than time sometimes.

Many times I saw demonstrations and uprisings and even terrorist activity. The best thing is to avoid it, of course, but sometimes I was in the middle of it before I had a chance to do something else. I praise God for His protection over me as I worked in that country. So many things I have to praise the Lord about and I have no fear to go and continue working there as God leads. Where He tells me to go, I will go, but I will wait on much confirmation for the exact timing and direction. This is so important for anyone who goes on foreign soil or anywhere for that matter. To be in the perfect will and timing of God is not hard if we rest in Him and wait on His prompting with much confirmation that comes through the prophetic Word and other means also. There must be a peace in our spirits and no fear or apprehension to open doors for doubts to come and deter us. God does lead us into what He has for us to do and we do not have to strive or be impatient. He prepares us for many different trials and sufferings we may go through. The "self life" must die so that He can have His way in our lives. He always provides where He guides I have heard it said.

Please pray with me if you have to deal with very difficult and dangerous circumstances in your life. God is able to give you peace in the midst of your storms.

Father, thank you for your wonderful, protective love covering me. I know that you care for me and will not mislead me in any way. I yield my will to you and choose to obey your plan for my life. I know that you created me with the desire to love and serve you with a joyful heart. Fill me with your peace and divine assurance that what you have required of me is what I will give to you in obedience. Keep me safe from all harm and danger and cover me with your armor to stand in the day of battle. In Jesus holy name I pray. Amen.

As you see God working in your life, you will grow in faith and continue to be a minister that He can work through. In His Word He has called all believers able ministers of the gospel. As we mature and gain capacity to live life in victory, we can help others.

Maturing in a process that causes us to learn wisdom from our mistakes and have the fear of God in our lives to do His will His way. We must never forget that He wants a mature "bride" and not a baby in diapers. He is the Lamb waiting for the bride to mature. The cost is to put our self-will to death and live surrendered to His will. The more we love Him, the easier it is to serve Him. We all know that we do not even see faults in someone when we are so totally in love. This is where that "love is blind" slogan arises I think. True surrendered love for the Lord is a beautiful thing, but to do His will we must be willing and rely on His grace. It is always sufficient for every task and test.

Being Obedient

At this time in our lives, my husband, Dennis, and I had our children grown and some were married. We continued working at our jobs and doing the work of the Lord. We changed churches in the city where we lived under the direction of God. It was a hard thing to do, but He clearly spoke of this change and the exact timing for it to happen. We did not understand all the implications of why this move was necessary, but He knew His plan for our lives. Some things are for a season and some things are for a lifetime. This was a season change for us.

We broke the news to the church and let the grace of God give us all strength to do what we must do. God had shown us that we were to go to a church that had just received a new pastor. We did not know this pastor or many in the church. It would mean starting all over again. We obeyed and went, not basing our decision on our own thoughts or reasoning. God would show us His reasons, which He did.

I did not understand the apostolic anointing that was beginning to surface in my life. This pastor needed those who would stand by his side and be a strength to him to help him heal a congregation that had gone through many trials. He was one that God would use to bring a new direction to the church. He and his wife had a big responsibility there as they began to make changes. God must give much wisdom in such situations and also will give grace as mistakes are made and lessons are learned. The rough edges began to be rubbed off, and the anointing began to flow. It was a training ground for me to die to self and let God handle the battles. My flesh wanted to scream over many things that happened in that church, but God was teaching me to pray and believe. It was a very hard trial for me to be in leadership there, but His grace was sufficient and I learned many things in the realm of the Spirit. God was faithful to show me how to pray and intercede that His body would dwell in unity and love. I continued to see the calling of God on my life take shape as I yielded my desires to Him.

Since my husband and I were elders in that church, we were invited to go with the pastor and his wife to a leadership conference in Oklahoma. I had such hunger for the Lord and I had grown so much from listening to seasoned men and women speak at conferences. I was excited and very anxious to go. My husband and I could make the trip by car in two days. We were combining this trip with another conference my husband had connected with his work. As we were driving to the Oklahoma conference, the Lord spoke to me so very clearly. He asked me to give up all my mission work in Guatemala. I was not sure that I wanted to hear that! I knew I did not want to hear that!

That's who I was, a missionary! I knew better than question the Lord and I certainly knew it was He talking. As I had this conversation in the spirit, I said to God, if that's what I must do, then I would do it. I just simply released this call on my life to Guatemala and was at peace. Then I heard the Lord say, I just wanted to know if you loved Me more than you loved what you were doing! I told Him, of course, I loved Him more. I had a gentle satisfaction that He really was first in my life. It was not hard to make that decision really. It was more of a shock to even think that He might ask me such a thing. Nevertheless, we traveled on and I related to my husband what just had happened. He thought it was very unusual.

We arrived at the hotel and met the others and I had completely forgotten what had transpired in the car on the way to the conference. We had such a good relationship with the pastors and other elders of the church. It was really fun to be together and especially at an international conference. One of the first nights there, a speaker who had been at meetings of Pastor Rodney Howard Browne was on the program. He told us that he carried that same anointing for releasing the joy. It was not long into the message before we all knew that the Holy Spirit was surely present in a very wonderful way. The laughter began to rise and there was a Holy Ghost drunkenness from the "new wine" of the Spirit. The joy and release in the Spirit was nothing like I had ever experienced before. It completely changed my life. That anointing was passed on to many that night and all went back to their hotel rooms so free and blessed.

The last day of the conference, the apostle over that organization had pastors and missionaries from other countries share for three minutes what God was doing in their ministry in their respective countries. I loved to hear them speak and listened intently to every word. It was awesome the miracles and signs and wonders that the Holy Spirit was doing using these ministers. Then a pastor and his wife from Peru, South America had their turn and as they began to speak, I went into a tremendous intercession in my spirit. I did not understand what was happening. Was God trying to tell me something about that country? I had such a burden for the people there and I began to sense a love for

63

that country and those pastors. I had never seen them before and watched where they went to sit after they were through speaking. The conference was over after that meeting so I had to talk to them to try to understand what God was trying to tell me in my spirit.

Every chance I got to go over and talk with them was thwarted because they were busy talking to others and I did not want to impose. I just came to grips with the fact that I may never know what that intercession was all about. As we were on our way out the door, there standing all by herself, was that pastor's wife from Peru. God is so good to do things his way. I immediately went over to her and told her how much I enjoyed her sharing about her work in Peru. I told her about the intercession and that I did not understand what God was telling me. She then said that maybe I would be coming to Peru. I did not know and just told her God would have to get me there because I had no clue to what He was doing. We parted ways and that was that.

We were all hungry so we went to a restaurant near the hotel where we were staying. We were seated by the hostess and then I looked up and at the next table to us was the delegation from Peru. The pastor's wife I had just talked to a few minutes before looked up and saw me sitting at my table. She came over to where I was sitting and put her arms around my neck and began to speak Spanish to me. I answered her in Spanish and then she said, "Maybe you are coming to Peru." Again I told her, God would have to put it together if He wanted me to go. She gave me her business card and I gave her mine. We ate and went back to our hotel.

I just pondered all this in my heart and prayed for the country of Peru since God had given me such a burden for the people there. Nothing like this had ever happened to me before.

For ten years I had suffered from a chronic infection in my body which was basically resolved with medication when I needed it for pain and discomfort. I had been told that there was a possibility that it was a type of cancer and had tests to reveal if it was so. The tests always returned negative. I never felt fear nor did I even share what the doctor had said with anyone. Even my family did not know. The doctor then proceeded to test me for a tumor which also proved to be negative. Still I had peace that all was well. The symptoms continued and were controlled with pills.

One day, about two months after the Oklahoma conference, I was sitting on the floor of my sunroom. It was December and very cold in North Dakota. I was praying and just spending time with the Lord is a quiet sort of way. All of a sudden I had a sharp pain in my abdomen and I was surprised. I had been taking my pills and should not have had any pain. One of the first things that I thought about was that I could not even go to Peru if the pills did not help me fight the infection and pain. Then in my spirit the Lord said that the pain and infection was a lie of the devil and that I should take authority over it in Jesus' name. Jesus has given all believers authority to rebuke the lies of the devil and stand on the truth of the Word of God. I told that lie to go and instantly the pain left. I felt it leave and I knew I was healed after ten years of doctoring with it and no one understanding why it was there. I rejoiced in the freedom from the pain and the freedom to know God was so faithful to me.

It was not even fifteen minutes later that the telephone rang. It was the pastor's wife from Peru and she was wondering if I could come and help them there for a while. I truly jumped for joy as I heard these words coming from so far away. God was so faithful in every way and now I understood why I must not go back to Guatemala. The whole direction of ministry was changing and this country was planted in my spirit in Oklahoma and now after much prayer and waiting on God, it was to be a reality that God was not through with me yet.

I told her I would come as soon as I could and told her surely it was the will of God. I had such an excitement in my heart and also an overwhelming peace that all was well. I shared with my family when they returned from work and we all knew that it was a new season in my life. I am so thankful for a supportive family, for without them, none of this could happen. I know that if God wants to do something, he needs someone to be willing, available and obedient to His voice. I had already promised God my faithfulness to serve Him in whatever way, in whatever place, at whatever time. I would be pleased to go and help those pastors in Peru and go I did.

CHAPTER 7

Peru

THE MONEY I NEEDED to go came in and I traveled to Lima, Peru in January of 1995. This country is in the southern Hemisphere so it is opposite from the United States. It was their summer and it was fairly warm being close to the equator. The pastor's wife from Lima met me at the airport. I looked for her in the crowd but she had somehow gotten a special pass to meet me before I went through customs and immigration. I was glad since I traveled alone and it was my first time in that country. I always prayed hard for favor going through new borders. All went well and soon we were off to her house on the other side of Lima. Lima has about 8,000,000 people living in or around it so it took us close to an hour even at the late hour that I arrived. By this time it was the middle of the night and I was very tired from the trip. It was an all-day and night affair because of the layover in Miami.

We went to bed only to get up very early the next day. I was to be live on a radio program. I had only been told the night before of this and had no idea what I would be asked to talk about in an interview. The lady who moderated the program was very nice and she wanted to ask me something related to the United States. In the newspapers at that time were articles discussing the death penalty in Texas. Would you believe I had to give my views on this topic! I really had not even thought about what views I had since I did not really have to deal with that issue. So I prayed that God would give me words to say that would help people realize that Jesus was able to change even the vilest sinner and criminal if they had an opportunity to hear the message of the gospel. I knew about the prison ministries we had in the United States that were bringing many to Christ. I tried to suggest without saying what opinion I had, that death is so final and there is no more chance to repent and be forgiven. If a person lived with a forgiven heart for the rest of his life in prison, he could tell so many others of Jesus' love. If he died a sinner, he was damned. If he died having given his life to Jesus, then he would pay the consequences here on earth, but have an eternal reward in heaven because of Christ's forgiveness of his sin. To me the issue was not whether to have the death penalty or not, it was to determine if he had a personal relationship with Jesus. Jesus died for sinners. Jesus already has paid the death penalty for us and now we can be forgiven and live life free from sin.

The pastor's wife was very pleasant and spoke very fluent English because she and her family had lived in the United States for about 20 years until God called them back to Peru to start a church there. She interpreted for me during the time I was there ministering. This allowed me a lot of freedom to share my heart. I loved to teach and preach, but the challenge was in doing it all in Spanish. God was certainly stretching me.

The city of Lima is very modern with many business and restaurant chains from the United States. The capital city is usually the only place in the whole country where one would see such chains. Over the time I spent working in Peru, I saw much growth and progress in many areas. The country is very diversified and has really three distinct areas which are the mountains, the coast, and the jungle. At the time I arrived, I did not even know that part of the Amazon jungle was in Peru. When I was told we were going to visit a church in the jungle, joy leapt within my heart. Could it be? Could it really be!

A national Pastors' and Leadership conference was scheduled to begin a couple of days after I arrived. Arrangements had been made for me to go and all my registration taken care of. It was held in a big stadium which was actually a bull ring with a dirt floor. This building was used for several events. There was a full house and also chairs were set up on the floor space. I was very privileged to be able to attend this wonderful conference. I met many Christian leaders from all over the country and also the speakers for the conference. The pastors I was staying with were key people and I was with them in the "waiting room" just before the time to begin. One of the pastor's there asked me how I liked the people of Peru and out of my mouth came something that totally shocked me. I said that I did not like them. Now this was not at all true and I corrected myself immediately with the truth. The pastor I was with was a little shocked too and wondered if I was joking around. I pondered what had happened in my heart as we went in to the conference.

While we were worshipping at the beginning, all of sudden I had a vision of a Japanese warrior dressed in black with no face. It was an evil sight and I immediately prayed that such a thing would be destroyed. I continued to worship and again I pondered this in my heart. What was God trying to tell me through all this? I began to have that same intercession for Peru that I had when I was in Oklahoma at that leadership conference. It was a very intense intercession and I knew God was "birthing" something in me through prayer. I felt so comfortable with these people and so happy to be in the country. It seemed that I was fulfilling a big part of my destiny in that place.

The main speaker was from Costa Rica and another speaker was from Mexico. I was able to completely understand what they said as they spoke in Spanish. My spirit was absorbing so much wonderful teaching from them. While the speaker from Mexico was briefly sharing about being glad to be in the stadium, she pointed at the back wall that had a large billboard showing the name of the stadium. It was named after the President of the country at that time. I did not know who the President of the country was and realized that he was from Japanese descent originally. This too I pondered in my heart. Things were beginning to be revealed to me. The conference continued and at the end, there was an altar call for those who wanted to respond to the message. I went forward among thousands of people. I was in tremendous intercession during this whole meeting and it was heavy upon me causing me to have a hard time even standing. It is difficult to explain except to say that it was similar to giving birth to a baby, only it was setting something free in the spiritual realm.

At the very end of all this, the speaker said that he had prophetic words for three people in the crowd and they were to come to the front of the platform to receive them. One of the words went to the pastors I was staying with who were not even able to go forward for the crowd, so he just spoke to them standing where they were. Another word went to a young man with a destiny in his country, and the last word went to me. Now, I knew God was up to something to pick me out of a crowd like that. That speaker had no idea who I was or where I was from. The word he gave me I have recorded on tape and it was a true word of prophecy to me revealing a ministry of intercession, training leaders and also having a prophetic mantle in my life. I fell to the floor under the power of the anointing which was so strong. When I was able to get up, still in the midst of this huge crowd gathered at the altar, I saw an older lady with a very crippled hand. I put my hand over hers and ran my hand up through her fingers which were all deformed. As I did, they all straightened out and we were both amazed and full of joy. A new anointing had been passed to me through that speaker and I began to have signs, wonders and miracles happen in my life. This surely was God increasing the ministry He had given me. I felt like I was being stretched to fulfill a purpose in Peru. I went back to the pastors' house that night very full of the night's events. It was an awesome experience for me to say the least.

I asked the pastor if I could share something with him of what had transpired with me. I told him about what I said and asked him if he was surprised I said I did not like the people of Peru. He said he was. I told him of the vision I had and also about the President being of Japanese descent. I said that God had shown me that someone in leadership of the country did not like the people of Peru and had a militant spirit against them and the President. He was so surprised to hear this from me who did not know anything about what was happening in the country. He told me that the President's wife hated the Peruvian people and they were in the process of divorcing. He understood that God had put intercession on me also for the country and the safety of the President. I continued to pray all the time I was in that country that there would be peace and freedom from strife. I had an intense battle inside me for the freedom of the country and wanted God to help the situation change.

The conference lasted several days with one day reserved for a women's conference. I was so blessed by the speaker from Mexico. She talked about being free from a spirit of control and manipulation. I listened and received conviction through her message. The Holy Spirit began to set me free from any form of control or manipulation in my life. I knew there was still a potential in me to do that. I knew that day that I was released from this spirit and was freer than I had ever been before. I was so free that I was "drunk with the new wine of the spirit" and could not even walk out of the building. Two strong men had to drag me through the stadium to the car. I seemed to always get "drunk in the spirit" when God would set me free from something. There is no other way for me to explain what I experienced except to relate it to the Acts 2 Pentecost experience. Supernatural things were occurring, but my mind was completely aware of what was happening. This was not some off the wall emotional show. I could not walk without help just as if I was drunk. Many times it has happened to me since and I have seen it happen to others everywhere I go. It is a biblical sign and wonder that God is pouring into His church today. The power of God is so strong that a person is not able to stand.

Many signs and wonders will be seen in the earth in the days ahead and the Bible will bear witness to them that they are from the Holy Spirit. The devil also manifests in certain signs and wonders and a person must be very discerning which spirit is in control. The true must be discerned from the counterfeit. This is what confuses many people and causes them to fear. God is a God who is supernatural and supernatural experiences will certainly occur even when we do not understand them. The Holy Spirit does not force anything on anyone. He sets people free to love Jesus.

Miracle Message

The pastors' house in Lima was very large with a large patio in the back. Up from the rear of this patio were steps surrounded by beautiful flowers and shrubs. At the top of the steps was a little house that had been partially burned out by a fire. It had a small room and a bathroom with a sink and a toilet. There was no water pressure up to the house so there was no water in it either. They put a big, plastic barrel of water in the bathroom to use to wash my hands in the sink and also to pour into the toilet to flush it. It wasn't a hardship for me to stay in that little house. I was very comfortable there and it was a good place to pray. The bed was comfortable, but there were many insects including a scorpion or two that I had to keep controlled. Everyday I had to clean the place well even shaking out my sheets which at times were full of ants. I got accustomed to living with the little critters and all was well. I really loved it there and the view was great. There even were more stairs up the back to a swimming pool which, of course, could not be used because there was no way to get water up to it without pressure. The cost of a pump was very high and it would have to wait until they could afford one. The little house was reserved for pastors and missionaries and I was honored to be in it while I was there. I came down to be with the family in the main house when I was not studying, praying or resting. I took my shower at the house and also ate with the family. I felt very much at home with them.

I had opportunities to speak at the church they pastored and also several other churches in the city. I was privileged to share on two or three different occasions at the 700 Club in Lima. God was using me to teach them about many things that would strengthen their relationship with the Lord and would bring them into a greater maturity in the Word. There were many manifestations of the anointing of the Holy Spirit to show them that God was confirming His ministry in the earth using those who are willing to be obedient to Him. I so loved to see people set free from old mindsets and also from fears and afflictions. I got to know so many wonderful people who were very receptive and kind to me. To this day I still return to visit with many of them when I have ministry in the country which has been every year for more than ten years now.

I will never forget one incident that happened while I was staying in "my" little house on the side of the hill behind the pastor's house in Lima. I had been asked to teach at the morning meeting at the church. I did not know what God wanted me to share with them and I went up to "my" little house to hear from God for a message. Nothing would seem to come. I realized that somehow I had picked up a "bug" from something I had eaten. That was very easy to do in a foreign country. I wasn't worried about it, but it kept me close to the bathroom! The barrel was full of water filled from a hose down below. The water was shut off when it was not being used. The family had gone to bed for the night and I still did not have a message. My "problem" began to get worse and I was visiting the bathroom often using up water at a great speed! I was beginning to get a little concerned about what I would do when the water was gone. I prayed and prayed and still I had no message for the morning. I was getting so tired and weak also from that "bug" I had picked up.

I cried out to the Lord to heal me now because the water was almost gone and I needed a miracle. I knew the enemy was trying to stop what God wanted to do. He wanted me to get discouraged because of how things were going. I refused to believe that God could not do a miracle for me right then. I quieted myself before the Lord and got peace in my spirit just as I used the last of the water. If I had to use the bathroom without water to flush the toilet, things could be rather foul in the room! I know that you can use your imagination to understand my dilemma. As I just chose to hear from God without being anxious, yet desperate, He told me to read Romans 8 in the Bible where it says all creation groans to be released from bondage. All of a sudden, I knew what to do. I thought if there was a bathroom in "my little house," then there must be water pipes leading up to it. There was no water pressure great enough to get water to the house without a pump below, but now I understood that God would cause the pressure I needed to make water flow up to the little house. I went outside and I prayed in the name of Jesus that creation be free and water flow through those pipes. There never had been water to that bathroom but I trusted God to do a miracle. I went back inside and prayed a prayer of faith for healing and then I felt a release in my spirit that I was healed. I praised and thanked the Lord for His provision. I went to bed without a message for the next day, but I fell peacefully asleep immediately.

About 6:00 in the morning, I awoke to a very loud noise. Where was it coming from? I got out of bed and went to the bathroom only to see water flowing out of the faucet that I forgot to close and the toilet tank was filling up. It was a miracle. I heard more noise coming from outside and I ran up the back steps to see that big pool which was about 9 feet deep filling up too. What tremendous water pressure God had caused! I rejoiced and danced with such freedom and victory to see how good God was to me. He had completely healed me and set creation free too.

The pastor's wife came running out from the house down below and yelled to me. Georgia, what is going on up there? Why, I asked? She said that there was so much water pressure in the house that she had to open all the faucets in the sink and bathtub in order to keep the toilet from overflowing when she flushed it. Hallelujah, God is good.

Now I had my message for the prayer service and it was straight from the revelation that God had given me. I was going to speak about the potential that lies dormant in each one of us and how God could release it for His glory and purpose. I understood now that there is a well in us that just needs faith and pressure to be released and the anointing power of God would flow through us.

I got dressed and went down to eat breakfast with the family and I shared the whole night's experiences with them. They were so excited to see the miracle. We all ran up to the swimming

74

pool and it was continuing to fill up. They could not afford to put a pump in to fill the pool so the family was never able to use it. Now everyone was going to go swimming that afternoon when we returned from church.

What happened at the meeting you ask? Well, God showed up big time. I shared about the events of the evening before and the spiritual truths behind them. God supernaturally opened spiritual wells that day. Living water flowed freely and the people were completely drunk in the Holy Spirit and dancing around like they were children again. This is what a refreshing of the Spirit does. Most of these people were in their 60's or more and what a blessing to see them free. God even entitled the message for them, POZO DE GOZO. It rhymes in Spanish and means WELL OF JOY.

But this was not all that happened. A lady had a big tumor on her side and another lady had clogged arteries and could hardly breathe. Both were totally healed and set free from physical problems. Miracles and more miracles happened. This is the God we serve showing us His mighty power. What I went through was worth every bit of the trouble to see His wonderful freedom and power change lives.

I will never forget that experience and I know they will not either. To God be the glory for all things He had done. It is so wonderful to do everything His way even when we haven't a clue what we are doing until He shows us. He always has a plan that will be far better than anything we could imagine.

Oh, by the way, years later, that pressure is still filling that bathroom in that little house on the side of a big hill in Lima, Peru. It's God's way of letting us know that He is still in control and gives us more than we could ever ask or think.

Joy In The Bull RING

I was asked to be one of the speakers for a women's prayer conference in one of the bull rings in Lima, Peru. I felt so honored to have an opportunity like that and God had the day planned. The bullring was not full by any means, but hundreds of people came

75

from several areas to be a part of this time. Many of the people were indigenous people who were dressed in their colorful attire and came with their instruments to pray for revival in the country. Lima was growing fast and had several million people with its surrounding cities. God has key people positioned all over the earth in strategic places to bring in the harvest of souls through prayer and evangelism. It is amazing how many people gather on short notice because God has given favor and influence to His anointed servants.

I went to the conference with a pastor and his wife who also interpreted for me when I spoke. There were many things that were scheduled for the conference so I enjoyed seeing and hearing all that occurred. The music at first was rather heavy since people did not seem to have much freedom in the Spirit. The Holy Spirit was beginning to be poured out in many of the gatherings with signs and wonders and releases evident. People were hungry to know more of what the Lord was doing by His Spirit. I prayed that God would bring victory to people and set them free to worship and praise with joy and freedom.

The night before I was preparing a message that God had put on my heart for the meeting. Usually I can just write down my notes all at one time when I get a message ready. That night God gave me the message in bits and pieces all night long. The lights were off in my room and I put a notebook by my pillow to write something if God woke me up and impressed some revelation on me for the message. In the morning I had to really study hard what I had written in the dark because it was all over the pages. In the scribbling I wrote was a revelation so astounding that I knew God was going to do something powerful at the conference. I felt God wanted me to share about David when he was doing battle with the Philistines in II Samuel 30. The leaders he was fighting under did not totally trust him and sent him back to a place called Ziklag where his home and family were. He and all his men returned to find their homes burned and wives and children taken by another enemy. All were devastated as you would imagine and wanted to stone David. Anger has to have release somewhere and it looked like a hopeless situation. But, the Bible said that David encouraged himself in the Lord. There was no one to go to and no one to encourage him. He had to find encouragement in God. God told him what to do and what would be the outcome. The account goes on and surely he recovered all and God gave them victory.

The Holy Spirit opened up that message with revelation and an anointing so strong that I was free to be very bold in the spirit. I began to sing in heavenly tongues of angels and the anointing flowed to the farthest corners of that bullring. The people were so set free that they began to rise and leave their seats to come down to the center of the ring and dance like they had never danced before. The Holy Spirit had encouraged them and strengthened them with new joy. The liberty that day was the greatest I had ever seen. The people recovered their joy and freedom from years of oppression, fear and unbelief. When joy comes, there is no question that people have received a release from oppressive captivity and bondage. The Lord showed the people that in the midst of what looks like a hopeless situation of poverty, sickness, and loss, He is able to do the impossible if they would only believe and focus on Him and what He can and will do. He is faithful and will never leave us or forsake us says the Word in Hebrews 13:5. Our situation can change around and be the greatest blessing we have ever known if we will rely on the Lord and obey His Word.

Toward the end of the meeting when we were ready to go home, the pastor who had put together the conference, told me that she had never seen an anointing so strong and so freeing as that. It was God showing His people that they haven't even begun to see the things He will do in days ahead to give them release and victory. What a day we live in and how great is our God.

One cannot be in Lima without seeing the many historic monuments and museums. There are many statues to commemorate great leaders and conquistadors. One such memorial to those massacred in the Spanish Inquisition is a huge Catholic Cathedral with Catacombs underneath it. It was a bizarre experience to walk through dark tunnels lit by only a single light bulb here and there and see pits full of human skeletal remains. These are the bones of many brave people who died for what they believed. I felt so much as I walked through these tunnels and wondered about those times of persecution in Peru.

It was quite an experience to see such parts of history. I also went into torture chambers that were mostly reconstructed to look like the originals. It was hard to imagine the cruelty that had been done to fellow human beings all in the name of religion.

Back at "my little house," in my sleep that night, I was awakened by an agonizing intercession in my spirit like I had never had in my life before. I was interceding in my language of tongues while sleeping. I woke myself up because of the groaning I was doing as I prayed. I asked the Lord what on earth was happening to me. He told me, and this so awesome to realize, that while I was in the catacombs, I had picked up through the blood of those martyrs, the crying out to God asking Him when He would avenge their blood. This is spoken of in the book of Revelation in the Bible. To think that innocent blood that was shed still was crying out to God for vengeance on their enemies! I hardly could take this in. It made me think of all those innocent people throughout history that have been slain needlessly. I thought about all those aborted babies and I knew that only God's mercy was sparing the judgment that should come. I learned that night how incredibly great is the grace and mercy of God to give the people space to repent before they are judged. Even when we destroy others with our mouths through hatred do we know that it's only the mercy of God that we are not destroyed. What a sobering revelation to understand such mercy.

I know that we do not realize what damage we may have done in our selfish moments, but God is a God that wants to avenge those who are wronged. He grants mercy to those who need mercy and always wants to restore relationships according to his love. The battle is not ours, but His and vengeance belongs to Him because He is merciful and just the Word says. Many times I see through His mercy that His goodness will break me and cut

78

me to the core as I see the selfishness of my own heart. I cannot help but repent that He would cleanse me from my sin.

If you are in need of understanding of how great is the mercy of God towards you, just ask God to show you what He sees that has not been repented of and put under the covering of His shed blood. As He begins to convict you of sin, you will see His mercy and know His goodness and love towards you to forgive your sin and cleanse you from all your unrighteousness.

Let's pray together asking God for a revelation of His mercy.

Gracious and merciful heavenly Father, thank you for your grace and mercy revealed to me through your unconditional love and patience. I know that I could not even live one day without your grace and mercy operating in my life. I need you, Lord, to show me more about your goodness and let me see what you see. Open the eyes of my understanding so that I may know wisdom concerning the truth of your abundant mercy and grace. Father, have mercy on me and cleanse me of all my secrets sins as I yield myself to you and receive forgiveness from anything I have done against my fellow man. I want to be merciful as you are merciful that I may reap mercy instead of judgment. In your holy name I pray. Amen.

Changed Lives

The taxis in Lima are everywhere and to go someplace in a taxi is quick and very reasonably priced. When I begin to speak Spanish to the taxi driver, it usually surprises them. They ask me where I learned to speak Spanish and I tell them I am a missionary and I learned some in college but mostly from being in the country speaking to people. From there the conversation could go any number of ways, but the result is usually the same. By the time I get to my destination, the man has repented of his sin and prayed the prayer of faith for personal salvation in accepting the Holy Spirit to be Lord over his life. I love to bring those taxi drivers into the Kingdom and sometimes I even see them again because they more or less have an area that they like to drive around in. This is what it is all about, isn't it? One more soul for Jesus and one less for Satan. To God be the glory for the marvelous ways He works in the hearts of men.

Terrorists

The Shining Path terrorist groups have had their day in the country of Peru and just about all the missionaries had to leave the country during this time. Now the country is under a democratic government and yet the terrorist groups spring up from time to time as they do all over the world. There was a group called the Tupac Amaru which had a goal of taking over the Congress and ruling the country. Somehow the authorities knew about the plot and stopped it before it could take place.

One night when the Pastors and I were returning back to the house after a church service, we saw vehicles backed up for miles. We tried to go an alternative route to get to the house and we experienced the same thing. We knew then that something was happening up ahead that was a major problem. We could do nothing but slowly inch ahead little by little. It took a very long time, but eventually we realized that the terrorists were barricaded up in a house in the neighborhood close to the pastor's house. When we got to the place, there was an armored tank sitting across the road from the house and many ambulances, police cars and special forces in the area. They had to fire on the house with the tank and automatic weapons while at the same time passing cars through between the tank and the terrorists. The terrorists had also taken hostages from the neighboring houses hoping to get leverage to negotiate.

When we drove through the battle zone, we all had to be on the floor of the car except the driver who lowered himself in the seat. We made it through safely as did most of the others. There were ambulances and sirens sounding through the night as well as flares being fired. I could see these events from "my little house" on the side of the big hill. I prayed fervently that lives would not be lost and for the capture of the terrorists. The next day we drove by the scene of the battle and saw all the shell holes in the house. I took a picture and it was almost the same as the picture in the newspaper. There were some injuries through all of the battle, the hostages were freed and all the terrorists were thrown into prisons in different places in the country. Among the prisoners was an America young woman who is still in prison at the writing of this book.

I thank God for His divine protection and covering. I thank God for swift justice and answered prayer. That was a little too close for comfort, but I know that it was for a reason that I was able to see something like that. I learned to pray more specifically for the problems in the country. These people are under terrorist threats more often than we know. Now that our country has experienced first-hand terrorist destruction, many of us pray more for the protection of God and trust Him to keep us out of harms way.

There was another uprising of terrorists who took over the Japanese Embassy when many delegations were inside. It was in the media worldwide. These terrorists wanted the release of the Tupac Amaru terrorists who were in prison. The special forces of Peru were able to kill or capture all the terrorists at almost one time. I was not in Peru when this happened, but had just returned from Peru two weeks or so before.

The times we are living in are times to be close to the Lord because we know not what will happen each day. We must continue to reach out to the lost and change the atmosphere of this world from hatred to peace by bringing the love of Jesus to the nations. God needs each one who will do his or her part. He is faithful to equip us and prepare us to be able ministers of His Gospel all over the world.

Lima is a big city and many missionaries and ministries are doing a great work. The country is starting to see many Christian churches raised up and working together to see the harvest in Peru come into the Kingdom of God. It is so good to work together to help and encourage the people there. There is a lot of idolatry and ancient culture there, but the One true God rules and reigns in the hearts of the people who have a personal relationship with Him. The violent past hopefully will not haunt them for the rest of their lives. Jesus wants to reveal Himself to these people who do not know Him as the Savior and give them eternal life in heaven with Him.

My husband went to Peru with me several times and was such a blessing to the people in the churches. He did not speak Spanish, but he spoke the language of love. We must realize that God's love will speak louder than words. The people were such a blessing to both he and I and will forever be in our hearts. Each year when I return, I want to see that my friends are walking in truth and are growing in grace and the knowledge of Him. It is truly a joy to be knit in the spirit with people from other nations and lands. We have seen great and mighty signs and wonders that God is doing in the midst of His people to set them free and to give them a hope for the future. We pray that the blessing of the Lord will make them rich in the wisdom of the Kingdom for the furtherance of the gospel. I can't imagine living my life without meeting those people in Peru. I would never want to miss out on the blessing of their relationship in Christ.

Arequipa

There is a large city in Peru called Arequipa which is located to the south in the Andes Mountains. There is a large church there that I usually work with when I am in Peru. This church and its leaders needed to be encouraged and established in more of what God was doing. God was moving in much joy and holy laughter at this time and the Holy Spirit set many people free from the bondages of hurts and offenses. It was so much fun to see the countenances change as the joy began to overtake them. The anointing was so strong at times when I was preaching, that several rooms of people fell under the power of the Holy Spirit. When I say fell, I want to clarify that no one got hurt as they slid down the stairs, slid off their chairs, dropped to the floor and even were stuck to the floor not being able to get up while under the power of God. This is where "spiritual surgery" took place as God began to heal the broken hearts and wounded spirits. So much abuse whether verbal or physical has been done to people. They have been victims of someone else's dysfunctional life.

There just isn't any greater joy to me than to see people get healed and set free. Out of ignorance many people have been trapped by past experiences and do not know that Jesus can heal and deliver them. The blood that He shed at the cross has power to set the captives free and we saw much deliverance as people learned to forgive and change. This takes the grace of God, but with the anointing and divine enablement of the Holy Spirit, it certainly happens.

We always stayed with a wonderful Pastors' family while we were in Arequipa and usually visit them each trip if we can. God gave one of the daughters in the family the English language almost overnight. She just understood it and was able to speak, read, and write the language very well. It is so good to see the signs and wonders of God in the lives of just ordinary people who love Him and believe.

People sent many items of clothing as well as teaching materials to the church in Arequipa. They were growing at a very fast pace as they met in their home groups. The youth were very active also inviting their neighbors, friends, and even strangers to the meetings in their houses. Each time that I returned I met so many new people who were recently added to the Kingdom of God. The excitement of new babes in Christ kept the church alive and full of joy. The church was very much of a training and discipling center there in the city.

As the church helped other small groups in other towns get a start, I would teach and train the people in the things of God. The anointing was always the strong point in my ministry to these people. God always ministered in such a supernatural way, that people received the impartation of the Holy Spirit and began to do things they had never done before. We saw many miracles of healing and the gifts of the Spirit operating as the people stepped out in faith and were used by God even in their families. This is the testimony that God is doing His work. The righteous fruit of the

Holy Spirit is seen in just ordinary people who love the Lord and are obedient to Him.

My husband loved to visit with the people in this place in the mountains because it was such an agricultural center of the country. He loved to walk through the fields of spices and other crops that were not grown in our country. He could communicate with farmers who attended the church in a language that only agricultural people would understand. This too is a sign to me. God used him mightily to lay hands on people and pray in English and they would be healed and set free. The Holy Spirit knows all languages and every prayer is understood. He realized that language is not a barrier in another country when the Holy Spirit does the work and God gets the glory.

This church is now entering into some of its most exciting days in the country of Peru. Many leaders have been raised up and the power of God continues to do miracles. The leaders of that church are now leaders in a greater way over several churches. God needs to just bring encouragement and support to people through those who will be available and willing to help them in their time of need. I feel like that is what I did with this church and its leaders through the anointing and the teaching gifts God has given me.

My heart is to see people go on into their destiny. God, even before we were born, planned out our whole life. He knows what shall become of us if we follow the leading of the Holy Spirit. This church in Arequipa was a big encouragement to me and I am so blessed to have had opportunities to be part of what God is doing there. The friendship I have with the Pastors' family is a special joy to me. These are quality people with a big responsibility to many people hungry for the teaching and ministering of the Word. I know God has a great ministry in that area through that church.

Sharing Jesus in the streets of Iquitos, Peru.

A typical
kitchen.

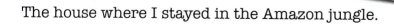

The house where I stayed in the Amazon jungle.

Tribal village
where tourists
can visit.

Waiting for the boat to arrive.

Church
discipleship
class.

Tarapoto (Mt. Jungle)

Bathing place, Amazon River inlet.

CHAPTER 8

The Amazon Jungle

THE DAY ARRIVED when the pastors from Lima would take me to the Amazon Jungle. We flew on a jet to the city of Iquitos. This was the capital of the area of Loreto, the largest area in the jungle. There was a pastor and his wife and family that lived in that city. Their house was very humble, but sufficient to provide shelter for the many who lived there. This family housed and helped many young people prepare for getting jobs, for Bible School and even some very young ones were given opportunities to attend a Christian school. There was a church there that had several other smaller churches under their covering and leadership in jungle villages. This church had trained many pastors, both men and women, to pastor churches in the villages where they lived. The training was not very adequate to say the least, but they did the best with what they had. Many Bibles were needed as well as study tools. Most of these villages were primitive by any standard. Some did have a generator that provided electricity certain times during the week, others did not. Some villages had a visiting doctor come now and then to help them with medical problems which were very serious. Malaria was in epidemic proportions in many areas that I went into. There were also other serious jungle diseases that we do not have in the United States.

I was so happy to at last be in the jungle. All I had seen thus far was the city, but it was surely a different world than the one I lived in. Certain areas in the city were modern enough for tourists to feel right at home in. By this I mean, there were hot showers, good food, air conditioning and decent beds to sleep in.

The group from Lima and I stayed in a three star hotel which was right in the center of town. It was comfortable and reasonably priced for my budget. To this day I still stay there some of the time I am in Iquitos. Most of the time I stay with the pastor's family who are pastoring in the central church that I work with in Iquitos. They have, like I said, humble accommodations, but the home was filled with the love of God. I would always choose to stay with them if I could. They have become family to me and the kids call me Tia which means aunt in Spanish. They called many friends of the family Tia, and I considered it a privilege to be called that.

Other areas in the city were so poor that the houses had dirt floors and no panes in the windows. The houses were basically one room and at night all slept in hammocks or on mats on the floor. Even the poor rob the poor there. There is much debauchery and a big drug problem. Cocaine is very easy to get and even legal to be used in its raw form in tea. People under the influence of these substances would often break into houses and harm the family sleeping inside. There really was no security because the shacks called houses were so vulnerable to intruders. But, life went on and there were no answers to the poverty and security problems. I tried to help some of the pastors who also lived in these wretched conditions. It always was a blessing, but I knew it was only temporary help. Encouragement, love and acceptance was the biggest blessing. I loved the people with a love that only could come from God. They were utterly poor, but managed to continue on with the hope of a better tomorrow. I became very close friends with many of the pastors and their families. I know some day I will not return and will not see my friends there ever again. Until God directs my paths to another country, I will continue to return and visit them in their affliction.

Adoption

The very first time that I went by plane to Iquitos, I saw out the window as we were coming in for a landing all the expanse of the river systems. There is an immense amount of

86

water flowing through the country and each river has a little bit different color from the other. The jungle is completely flat in the area around Iquitos and one can see for miles. The airport was kind of what I expected to see in the jungle. All the bags were handled by hand and there were no conveyor belts for anything. Strong boys would have jobs at the airport when a plane arrived. They were not paid a salary, but survived on the tips the passengers gave them. They especially wanted to help foreigners because they knew the tips were much better. Today the airport has been modernized. Many tourists also traveled to the jungle to go on river cruises. Some were very modern and others were just enough rustic that it would be an adventure, but the boats would have reasonable accommodations and safe water and food so that no one would worry about getting sick.

The pastor of the church and his family were there to greet us. They were very friendly, but spoke basically no English. They were very pleased, to say the least, that I could speak Spanish. Without the Spanish language I never would have been able to have all the adventures that I had. God had his hand in that way back when I was in high school and gave me the desire to take it up in college as a teaching career. We were taken to a hotel where we had a comfortable place to stay. I loved everything that was there and the joy inside me to be there was not explainable. God was giving me the desires of my heart and fulfilling my dreams. I had waited over thirty years to see this day.

After a few days of being there, I had time to visit at length with the pastor and his wife. Their schedule is incredibly busy and they are involved in so many areas. I remember we were sitting in a restaurant that I really liked just talking about various things going on with the ministry. The pastor and his wife had just returned from a place way back into the interior of the jungle many days journey by boat. It was a place that was very primitive and had many problems with disease. There was a good church started there and it was doing well. The pastor began to tell me about a little girl around two years of age that they brought back with them. She had lost her mother who was only nineteen years old to malaria. The little girl also had malaria and was not expected to live unless she got medical help. Even with help, it was doubtful if she would live. She had parasites and amoebas also plus deficiencies in many areas. The grandparents wanted the pastors to take the little girl back with them to Iquitos and get her well. The grandparents asked them if they would adopt her since her mother had died. The grandparents had no choice but to send her back with the pastors or she would surely die. The pastors had a big decision to make. They knew she would need to be in the hospital to get well. The pastors had six children of their own and they could not afford any more or the cost of the hospital stay plus the medicine that she would need to get well. They prayed fervently for God to show them what to do.

At the time we were talking, the little girl was in the hospital in very serious condition and very thin. The hospital was not equipped to handle every kind of situation and she had to have an answer to prayer to be healed. The pastor felt that he and his wife would have to find someone to adopt the little girl. There was no way to pay the medical costs and if someone would adopt her, all the expenses would have to be paid by the ones adopting.

During the conversation, my heart was beating hard as I could not believe what I was hearing. God was doing something so wonderful and He had ordained it to come to pass in this way. The pastor asked this question. Do you know any good Christian couple who would want to adopt this little girl not knowing if she would even live or not? What a tough question he thought.

I was so excited by this time I could hardly contain myself. You see, right before I left North Dakota to go on the mission trip to Peru, a nice couple in my church there spoke these words to me. If you find a child that we could adopt there, please do something to indicate that we are interested in adopting. They trusted me to hear from God and know what to do. So you see how God made a divine connection two continents apart for such a time as this. This timing was as perfect as it could be. God is never early and He is never late. No man could have orchestrated this. It was a "God thing!"

I told the pastor and his wife about the couple and what they had said to me before leaving for Peru. But under these circumstances it would have to be a decision made by a Word from the Lord to them. It meant they would have to begin sending money for medical expenses immediately to give her what she needed to get well. There was no guarantee that she even would get well. The hospitals in third world countries almost always want the money in cash up front or they cannot provide the care that is needed or do any medical procedures. I asked if I could go to the hospital to see her and take a picture of her for the couple. I wanted to pray for her recovery too. That was impossible since she was so critical. The pastor and his wife were the only ones allowed in to see her. I gave them my camera and told them to take some pictures of her and I would take them to the couple in North Dakota and see what would happen. We all prayed and knew down deep in our hearts that this little girl would live and see her destiny realized. God didn't bring her that far to let her die, we thought.

When I returned home I shared with the couple in North Dakota about the situation and asked them to pray about what to do, but that a decision had to be made as soon as possible. At first they did not know what to do because they had just purchased a house and they did not have the funds for such expenses at their disposal. They decided not to adopt this little girl with all the complications. They continued to pray for clarity though because they did not have total peace that they had made the right decision.

One cannot just base decisions on the situation, the state of one's finances, or logic when destiny depends on one hearing from God and His perfect will being done. When there is no peace after a decision is made, then something needs to be adjusted to fit into the perfect will of God. A short time later, the couple called me and told me that they were sure God wanted them to adopt this little girl and would begin to send money to the pastor's account to pay for medical costs so she could receive all the treatment she needed to get well. I was overjoyed, and I knew God was doing something very special for all concerned.

The news was welcomed by the pastors and they knew that God had answered the prayers in His way and timing. Adoption proceedings were begun to do all the process legally on both ends. The adoption process was not very easily done in Peru since it had to go through Lima which was only easily reachable from Iquitos by plane. There were many times the pastors called me to pray because the situation looked impossible. The pastors had to do something that they had no knowledge or understanding of. The legal process is very complicated and foreign to those who have never dealt with it. God intervened time after time. We were doing something with this adoption that had never been done before in the jungle. We said to the lawyers, "We want this little girl to go to that couple in North Dakota." They were not accustomed to do this and it took three years before the process was complete. It would take a whole book to explain all that happened during those three years. God was in control of the whole process though and the results were realized. The little girl was finally well and given permission to leave the country after three years of medical treatment. This was a walk of faith on the part of the couple in North Dakota and on the part of the pastors in Peru. Those were times when one just trusted God and moved ahead with determination to do what God wanted.

I had gotten to know the little girl quite well from the many trips to Peru while the process was taking place. She was told of her future with the couple in North Dakota and prepared as well as a five year old could to go to a strange new place and climate. She was very excited to go and yet very sad to leave the only family that she remembered. It would be sad for all when she left, but God gave them all his grace and comfort to make the transition. The adoptive parents had to spend almost six weeks in the country with the little girl to see if there was a bond and if all would work out. But, one day, the final approval to leave was given. The parents spoke very little Spanish and the little girl almost no English. It was a challenge, but it was the will of God for it all to work out.

When the parents arrived back in North Dakota with the

90

little girl, it was the winter season and she had never experienced temperatures that cold before. They had bought her a parka and she was ready for her first adventures in the United States. I was at the airport to welcome them when they arrived. She was scared and tired when she arrived, but when she saw me, she recognized me from being at her house in Peru and ran into my arms. I got such a big hug and her face broke out into a smile that someone familiar was still in her life. What a blessing it was to me to see everyone so happy. I did not know when the adoption would be final or when they would be coming back with her. My husband and I were moving to Florida just three weeks later and I didn't want to miss her arrival in North Dakota. God had it all worked out and we were able to see her several times before we left and take lots of pictures to show the family in Iquitos that all was working out just wonderfully. It was hard for her to put things together at first because she had seen me in Peru and then I left Peru. She did not know where I went and then she traveled so far from Peru and found me again in North Dakota. Now I was going to leave again for Florida.

Each year I returned to North Dakota and she always remembered me. She learned English quickly and adapted to her environment without much trouble. Children are so flexible. I hoped I could be so flexible as she. I always took pictures to take with me when I returned to those pastors in Peru and they were so happy that she was adopted into a wonderful Christian family and could be all that God wanted her to be. What a happy ending to years of waiting and believing God to give them the desires of their hearts.

One of the last trips I made to the jungle, I was at a conference in a village five days out from Iquitos. This area was not so far from the area that the little girl was from. I met her grandparents there who had traveled by boat to the conference. I also met her aunt and her baby. I dedicated publicly this baby to the Lord at a church service. I was able to tell the grandparents, after several years of wondering what happened to their granddaughter, that all was well and God had it all planned out from the begin-

ning. They were so pleased that she recovered and had a good
family to raise her and give her what she never would have had in
the jungle. I hope one day she can visit her family in the jungle
and see where she lived before and understand how good God was
to give her a such a destiny. I know God has more in store for the
people involved than I could even imagine. His ways are above
our ways and who can understand it all from an earthly perspective. It's things like this that cause my faith to grow. God always
looks out for His creation if we will allow Him to have His way
and obey His voice.

Ministry Continues In Peru

The church in the city of Iquitos had prayer and fasting
days at least once a week. These were times when all who could,
would gather and spend the day praying, worshipping, dancing
before the Lord with the tambourine, and someone would teach
the Word. God did many awesome signs and wonders at these
meetings using the spiritual gifts that were in the people. Giftings
like the Word of Knowledge and Wisdom, Prophecy, Healing,
Faith, Miracles, Tongues and Interpretations, and others were
exercised. These gifts are spoken of in I Corinthians 12 in the
Bible. I loved to teach the people how to "flow" in these spiritual
gifts God had given them. They were becoming bolder and more
confident to step out in faith and share what God was putting on
their heart. Astounding revelations were voiced and God showed
the church the direction it should go using these spiritual gifts.
God is a discerner of the heart and knows what attitudes need to
be dealt with so the church could go forward into her destiny.
When God speaks through His people, it is a holy thing that is
happening. All were learning to hear the voice of God in their
spirit and share the Word.

One such time in one of these prayer meetings was very
exciting. For some reason, God told me to go to Peru, but not to
tell anyone there I was coming. I had never done it that way
before. So I obeyed God and arrived in Lima. I did not know what
He wanted me to do. As I prayed, the Lord showed me first to go

to the mountains and visit the church there. I bought my ticket and took the bus the next day. This was the first time I had taken the bus, because usually I flew. We had many items of clothing that people in the United States had sent with us so we took them by bus to save money. The timing of God to place us exactly in the right place at the right time is so amazing. If we will hear His voice in our spirit, He will lead and guide us every step of the way. I loved to hear God and follow His instructions to me. If He sent me, then He would show me what to do.

God spoke to my spirit to go first to the city of Arequipa in the Andes Mountains. The Pastor and his family were very glad to see me. I stayed at a hotel the first night because they did not know I was coming and I did not want to shock them. I called them to say I was in town and they were so excited and insisted I come immediately to stay at their house. It was so good to have such a welcome. I stayed about two weeks there with them and the Lord did many wonderful signs and wonders by His Spirit to set the people free. Encouragement is so important to these people and I love to see them grow in Christ. I was able to do much teaching in the smaller groups and this is fun for me because I get to know more people in a closer way. They impart many things into my life too.

I returned to Lima and felt in my spirit to go immediately the next day to the jungle to visit the church there. When I arrived, all were surprised to see me since they did not know that I was coming. They had a prayer meeting the day before and someone had stood up to speak what God had put in his spirit. He said that Georgia was in the country and would be in Iquitos the next day. He could have only known this by God showing him. This was not something that he had ever done before nor had I ever arrived without notice before. When I truly did arrive, there was much excitement, not only to see me, but because the supernatural revelation of God had showed them the thing before it had happened. They were realizing that God could tell them how to pray, when to speak, and what to do in every situation. The timing of God is always perfect if we will just listen to Him and obey what He tells us to do. This is called walking in the spirit so we do not lean to our own understanding in our fleshly thinking. The church must learn to walk according to the Word God gives or it will not accomplish all that it was sent to do. God will always show us what the next step is and expect us to take it in faith trusting Him all the way.

When I stay at the pastors' home that is near the church, I get to meet many interesting people who come by to see the pastors. One evening while we were sitting around the table talking, a family came to visit. I had never met them before, but could see that they were very discouraged and broken in spirit. It was a pastor, his wife and several children who had been deep in the jungle as missionaries to the people in the interior. As I listened to what they were saying, I knew God was telling me that He would change their lives and restore them. You see, they had lost their oldest son while they were serving God in the far corners of that jungle. He died of malaria as do so many because there are no doctors or any kind of medical help. The family was devastated over this and was not even able to function as missionaries at this time because they had sunken into despair even of life and did not understand why God would allow this.

I laid my hands on them and began to pray as the power and anointing of God flowed through me. That spirit that had them captive trying to keep them from ever ministering again was broken and freedom and release came. Joy returned and healing of all their emotions restored them to even a greater relationship with the Lord. They had seen that God was not behind this, but that the devil was deceiving them into thinking that it was not worth the sacrifice. God used their testimony in years to follow to help so many others back to a place of trusting God. The enemy is very active in witchcraft and deception to destroy the ministers of God. I too have had to do spiritual warfare to break curses assigned against me by witch doctors. Now this pastor is a powerful apostle to the tribes in those interior churches that are being raised up. He is seeing God do many mighty miracles to heal the people as the demonic forces are brought down by the authority of the Word of God. The power of God is greater and able to break off the curses that often manifest through the spirit of death.

Once when I was preaching in a village church, a man walked in the back of the church and all of a sudden I knew that I was dying. I could not breathe and began to cough and almost crumpled to the dirt floor of the church. I realized that this was no more than a curse that had been thrown on me by that man who was a witch doctor. In my spirit I prayed in the name of Jesus for that curse to fall off me and instantly I regained my strength and continued to preach. This all took place in a matter of seconds. How fast we can die if we do not understand the power of the name of Jesus in the believer who knows his authority in God. God often allows such a display that the power of God can be manifest to destroy the works of the devil. Greater is He that is in us, than he that is in the world says the Bible. The people know that darkness cannot overpower the light of Jesus. Spiritual truths are better demonstrated to the people than spoken. God knows that they will understand much better through a real encounter with Him. The people are afraid of the witch doctors because of their supernatural powers. Their power comes from Satan while the greater power that the Christians have comes from God.

Many times I had encounters with that spirit of death. I recognize it now and it also knows who I am. Life will not be snuffed out if people have the authority of Jesus in them and cast out this spirit of death.

There was a time in Lima when the pastors took me to the hospital to see a lady who was very sick with cancer and had surgery. She was in the intensive care unit and I was allowed to go in as a minister. When I entered her room, all I could sense was death in the air. The lady was very pale and weak and could only talk in a whisper. The pastors introduced me to her and I asked her some questions. The Lord immediately gave me a Word of Knowledge what had opened a door to this spirit of death that I knew was on her. I asked her if she had been divorced before and if she was in a relationship with someone now. She said that she had been divorced twice and was dating someone at the moment. I told her the Lord had showed me that she had a fear of relationships and that she felt trapped in the one she was in and had asked God to let her die rather than enter into another marriage. She was astounded that God had told me this and agreed that it was true. I wanted her to know that God had put the relationship she was in together for her and that she would not die, but live and would be out of the hospital in two days totally well and free to marry. We prayed and that spirit of death was broken off of her. Her countenance immediately changed as color came back into her face. The whole atmosphere of the room became light and cheery and joy began to give her strength. She sat up in bed and knew that she was healed and delivered from death. We all rejoiced to see the power of God set people free from demonic strongholds.

I often thought how marvelous it was that God could use me in someone's life like that. He brought me all the way from North Dakota at that specific time to pray for that specific person who had a specific purpose from God. Death had to flee and life came more abundantly through the supernatural power and revelation of God. God is looking for anyone who is willing and available to lay his or her life down to serve Him wherever He would desire. We must die to our desires and live to do His will. This is a choice that all believers have. How many will be obedient to the calling He has on their lives? It is the anointing and the spiritual gifts that do these things. In ourselves we have no power set people free. We must discern what is from God and what is from the devil. False anointings and spiritual gifts are used by the devil to destroy. These are not days to be ignorant of his devices says the Lord. We can be destroyed from lack of knowledge. It is not a light thing to be a servant of the most high God. He is demonstrating His power in the earth, but He must have people who will yield to the Holy Spirit and be his ambassadors of righteousness. All is to glorify God and not ourselves. He is the One who does the miracles. He will teach us of His ways as we learn to listen to His voice and obey.

One day back in Iquitos in the jungle, the Pastor's wife and I were just visiting in the house when a knock came at the door. It was a small framed lady who was desperate to talk to us. She knew that a missionary was there and asked if we could come immediately to her house. She had a daughter about 10 years old who was dying. The doctor had sent her home to die. She had a catheter in her bladder and had lain in bed for four days without eating or drinking. The doctor could not heal her. She was a twin and her sister and family stood around the bed crying and praying for God to send someone to heal her. I felt like I was in the book of Acts in the Bible and God was using me the way he used the disciples.

That morning I had preached to the church about moving our faith. I did not think that I would be tested so quickly on what I had preached. I thought, if God was putting me to the test, then it was to show me and others that He surely will do what is needed to set people free. The girl was obviously in a coma and I could not speak to her, but must speak to her spirit. I laid my hand on her and in the name of Jesus commanded her to arise and be healed. I told the spirit of death to leave. She sat up in bed, but I could see she was still in a coma. God had spoken to her spirit and she responded. All the family was surprised. I asked them to bring me a soda bottle with some water in it. I put the water to her lips as I held her steady and she drank a couple of drops. In my spirit I knew she would live. I boldly told the family to have someone get up every hour or two during the night and give her water to drink from the bottle. I would come back the next day and check on her, but assured them she would be fine.

The next day I returned and she was lying in bed. I could tell she was sleeping normally and not in a coma. The family said that she drank two bottles of water during the night as well as a little soup broth. I did not wake her, but I restated that God had healed her and she would be just fine in a short while.

The next year when I returned to Iquitos, I asked of this little girl who had been in a coma. The pastor's wife said she was completely healed, normal and there were no problems with her whatsoever. We rejoiced that God is so good and so faithful to do signs, wonders and miracles as proof of His Kingdom being on

97

the earth today. It was a testimony to the people there of the true and living God. This was so necessary because of the witchcraft that abounded in this place. I love to see the works of the devil destroyed by the anointing and Word of God.

So many times we would be sitting in the house sharing about the things God was doing all over the world and a knock would come at the door. It would be another person asking us to come to her house and pray for someone who was sick and dying. So many times we saw the power of God heal and deliver people from their situations. There must be the power of the Word of God revealed so that the Christian life does not become form. If God's power is not in His Word then we do not understand what authority we have been given by Him to do the works that Jesus did while He was on the earth. This very power is available to believers today. God is faithful to His Word and cannot lie. The problem lies with us to believe and by faith do what He commands us to do.

For some of you reading this book, these things sound very strange. But, if you will believe that Jesus Christ is Lord and is the same yesterday, today and forever, you will understand that miracles are happening all over the earth today. God has poured out His Holy Spirit on all humanity to do the impossible. It is through the power of the Holy Spirit and yielding to this power that the world will know that surely Jesus is alive. This is of the utmost importance to win the lost to Jesus. If He is not alive and doing wonders through his people, then our faith is in vain. He is alive and we do believe and will see many manifestations of His life in us.

I would like you to pray this prayer with me if you have desired to know the resurrection power of the Lord. It is the power of the Holy Spirit to set the captives free, the power to heal and restore, the power to bring life and even raise the dead. Yes, the dead are being raised by this same power of the Lord. You will hear of it for it is surely happening in the world today.

Lord Jesus, I cannot in my own strength do anything. I thank you that you have given me life and the authority of your Word. I humble myself before you now to ask you to cleanse me of my unbelief and doubt. Forgive me for not understanding that you live in the hearts of believers and will do signs and wonders through your Holy Spirit today. I give you permission to fill me with this power of the Holy Spirit with signs and wonders following me because I believe. Guide me into all truth and keep me from bringing any glory to myself because it is only you that deserves the glory. I praise your mighty name and thank you for the gifts you have given me. In your powerful name I pray, Amen.

There is a song that the Lord had given me several years ago. It says what my heart understood of the power of the Lord at that time.

The power has come to change our lives
The people of God will arise
We will all be saved alive
It is done in the name of Jesus.

The King has come to proclaim His name
His power will demonstrate His fame
Touched by God, we are never the same
It is done in the name of Jesus.

The name of Jesus is lifted up
We His people will drink the cup
We go in His power and never give up
It is done in the name of Jesus.

Our sins He bore upon the tree
When He died for you and He died for me
How else could we have victory
It is done in the name of Jesus.

We receive what He has done
We've been cleansed by the blood of the Son
Surely we know that He's the One
It is done in the name of Jesus.

In the name of Jesus
In the name of Jesus
Done by the Son, the victory won

All in the name of Jesus
All in the name of Jesus
All in the name of Jesus.

CHAPTER 9

Be On Guard

I LOVED TO MINISTER in the church in Iquitos. The people were so receptive and God always did something unique in the meetings. There was one night when I was preaching and all of a sudden over the side of the building, between the roof and the wall, rocks started to fly towards me. I didn't know if I was preaching good or bad to deserve rocks. The one thing I did know was that the devil did not like it. I knew that stones were thrown at the disciples when they were preaching, but this was just me. These were not pebbles, but rocks bigger than baseballs.

I felt in my spirit that we were really breaking through in the spiritual realm, and the devil had to do something to destroy the anointing and wreak havoc in the meeting. I could see the people in the service were wondering what I was going to do. They maybe thought I would be offended and never come back with treatment like that from the outside. They did not know that I was not afraid of anything and this certainly was mild compared to other distractions I had faced.

I began to rejoice and declare that the devil was defeated and this only proved that we would have victory and freedom that night. The people began to receive joy as I said nothing would stop me from ministering to them. I did not have any fear of the devil because I knew he was not going to rob the blessing those people needed that night. As joy and liberty broke out, people came out of their seats and starting dancing in groups of three with arms hooked together. They celebrated the authority we have as believers and rejoiced in the Lord. The night was a total success and people were delivered from bondages of fear, anger, jealousy, unforgiveness, and more. The message I had preached went right along with the demonstration of how God sets us free when we respond correctly to the Holy Spirit. I really stand at awe when I see the Holy Spirit not only give revelation to the Word, but also do something practical so the people can see it in action. If we keep our attitudes right and discern in the spirit what really is happening, we will stay on course with God and many will see the glory of the Lord.

In the middle of the night while I was sleeping at the pastors' house, I heard a bunch of ruckus in the living room. I thought that maybe the boys had brought some friends over to pray or some such thing. I was tired so I just stayed in bed and went back to sleep. When I went out for breakfast in the morning, the family was discussing the events of the night before. It was a serious, yet humorous capsulation of what went on. It happened that while the boys were still up yet at about 2:00 A.M., a young robber entered the house through the back door. The boys heard him and were ready to surprise him when he entered. One of the girls also heard the racket and got out of bed to see what was going on. This young robber was high on drugs or alcohol and was bold enough to go into a house with people inside. There was no fear of the Lord there to even rob a pastor and his family. This person had tried to do this, and had succeeded to steal a few things before. What happened is the humorous part.

I thought it was pretty clever of them to even think to do this. The boys held him down on the floor roughing him up a little, but not hurting him too badly while their sister got a scissors and cut one half of his hair off and one eyebrow. Everyone in his family would know that he had been up to no good and was fortunate to have escaped with only his pride wounded. It taught him a lesson and I don't believe to this point he has ever tried to do it again. They did not report him to the authorities, but had mercy on him hoping that he would change his ways and come to a personal relationship with Jesus. Just the fact that his eyebrow would take a long time to grow back would raise a lot of questions in his family about what might have caused that to happen. I pray that he will understand that crime does not pay and there is a better way to live life.

So many interesting and educational things went on while I stayed with those pastors. I saw how renovations were made in the houses there. This family wanted to put a second floor on the house so they bought the materials and had them all brought, not only to the house, but also into the house. Nothing could be left outside because it would not be there the next day. Some of the big pile of sand used to make cement even disappeared. I suppose if there had been room in the house, it would have been in there too.

Now what do you suppose they used for the framework of the second floor? In the jungle, there are no two by fours like we use. No, they use small tree trunks from a certain kind of tree. Of course, they were not straight, but there can be allowances for that somehow. There were big piles of those trees in the living room. You might think that is not so bad. But, those trees were full of little insects that began to roam around the house and get into beds and chairs. It was not so terrible, yet it caused some discomfort.

Cement blocks were also carried into the house and filled up one and one half rooms. This house was not that big and the family was made up of eight people plus a couple of girls who helped with the chores and myself. We stacked those blocks in one room and then when the trees were nailed into place for the structure, we had to move them to another room and stack them. We did this more than once. There was no easy way to do things in that country. Everything had to be moved around with every room that was prepared with the supporting structure for the second story. I had to take lots of pictures of this ordeal, because I knew that people in this country would have not ever seen such a way of building. The next year when I returned, all was finished. They did not have enough money to finish more that just the second cement floor and redo the roof. The roof was made of corrugated tin. It went all the way across the house and completely covered all the rooms. The wall now went all the way up to the ceiling and no one from next door could look over the wall into the house. Yes, there were many drawbacks to living in houses there because there was one common wall between the houses and a roof that allowed for air to circulate.

There are two seasons in the jungle as far as I am concerned. They are hot and hotter! The first few years I stayed with that lovely family, the house had a roof that only partially covered the rooms. Part of the dining area was open to the sky and when it rained, it rained in the house. There were always large, plastic barrels set in that place to catch the rainwater to use for their showers. There was no running water, just water from a hose outside or rainwater. If you wanted a shower, you just used a pitcher to pour that rainwater over your body and, voila, you got clean. The room where I slept was off the dining area and the bathroom was across the room from that. If it was raining in the night and I had to make a trip to the bathroom, I would get wet. I just chuckled about it, because I was so glad to be staying with them in their house. The pastors and I always joked about the accommodations they had. They called it a seven-star hotel because one could just look up and really see the stars! I have so many fond memories of that house and family and look forward to seeing them each time I go back to Peru.

One of the sons had a motorcycle that one of the missionaries helping them had bought so he could get to work easier. That motorcycle also was in the house at night. The last trip to their house had some fun additions. They had two parrots from the jungle and they could talk. One of the parrots knew each person's name in the family and could utter it very plainly. This was very interesting to me and I enjoyed those birds and the amazing things they could say. It kept them talking right so the birds only learned good words! The birds talked even in the middle of the night so there never was a dull moment.

Much evangelism is done in the streets there in the city of Iquitos. When mission groups from the United States came down to help the church, many souls were added to the Kingdom. It seemed that without effort the people would accept the Lord into their lives personally making Him Lord. In our country we really do not know how much we need the saving grace of Jesus working in our lives. We have so many places to go and so many things to do. The people who have nothing know they need hope of a better life. Jesus is the answer we all are looking for. Only He can fully satisfy us with the help we need to overcome our battles for survival.

Churches are springing up all over the city now as pastors are getting trained and people are helping them reach their own people better. The education they get is not sufficient, but they work with what they have. Their relationship with the Lord is strong and they must believe by faith that God will supply all their needs as the Bible says. Every day they are put to the test. There is no other way because the jobs that are available pay very little and many struggle to even feed their families. There is no government help for them. Faith in God does provide miracles as they pray and trust Him for every day.

Visions Of God

When teams of leaders gather to train and help the people, the purpose is to give them new vision and a greater vision of God and His ability to get them where He wants them to go in the spiritual realm. All eyes must look to the harvest of souls that are ready to come into the churches. The churches must be ready to receive this tremendous ingathering. The maturity level of leaders has to rise. What do I mean by that? I mean that the mature body of Christ should be able to handle problems better because of much teaching and practical experience. There are mentalities "out there" that will accept the status quo as the norm and this is not so according to God's economy. If the mentalities change because of the Word of God speaking truth into people's hearts, then the stage for miracles is set. Seeing God as a God who is present in us, doing work through us, and affecting people around us is a necessity for each of us to increase our faith and trust in Him. He is looking for a generation who will let Him be God as He wants to be God. Our mentalities should never limit us in any way when it comes to what God wants to do in the earth today.

Maturity will accept the truth of the Word, believe it, and act on it. God is relevant to society today and will demonstrate His power to break poverty and lack off of it. Someone once said that it is not great faith in God, but faith in a great God that gets the job done. He will always use our "little" to give us His "big."

If people do not realize that God dwells among them in their spirits, then God is never to be experienced in His totality. If it does not work for the United States, then it does not work we think. This mentality has to go and God's mind that is in us must dictate our thoughts and actions. We truly do have the mind of Christ in us because it says so in the Word. Can you imagine what life would be like if we would just understand what treasure we have in these earthen vessels! The Word says that He is greater in us than what is in the world trying to hold us back or distract us to think otherwise. This "otherwiseness" has got to go so that we get the spirit of an overcomer into our mentality. Without the message to people "out there" that Jesus in us overcomes all things, I have no message. I preach of the Jesus who does overcome and who transforms us to think like He does. He says nothing is impossible to those who believe on His Word. If a person believes, that person is able to enter into a spiritual dimension that affords all the possibilities of heaven to be visible in this present world. The reality is that Jesus reigns with authority and power and we know now that He is in us as this reality. If He reigns, then we reign with Him and His Kingdom has come to earth.

I hope you will open up your heart and take this into your life. Pray with me, if you will, for God to show you His way of thinking.

Father God, all of heaven waits to see the manifestation of the sons and daughters that you have birthed into this earth. I pray that you will be glorified through me in all of my thoughts and actions. Cause me to let go of religious thinking that is only a form without power and set me free to see with my spiritual eyes the mysteries of your Kingdom that has come to this earth. I pray, Thy Kingdom come and Thy will be done on earth as it is in heaven. Let this prayer not be mere words without power, but a mighty understanding of your heart when You taught me to pray this way. Forgive me for making You be what I understand you to be in my limited thinking. I now give you permission to change my understanding of who You are and who I am in You. Thank you, Lord for revealing new truths to me and setting me free to know You as you would have me know You. Amen.

CHAPTER 10

A Word In Season

P ROPHECY IS A WONDERFUL SPIRITUAL GIFT to the people of God to speak forth the revelation of His Word to us today. It is not as mysterious as it seems, only to those who do not understand what God has given us. Certainly there are abuses in this area as well as in other spiritual gifts. The Apostle Paul had to address churches about this very thing to teach them how to use and receive this revelation through prophecy and other spiritual gifts. These gifts are given to the body of Christ so it can profit from fresh revelation that agrees with the Word and what God is saying today. These gifts are not to cause confusion or to be wrongfully exercised. This is why there must be teachers to explain what God is doing as He releases His church to be effective in the world today. Without His voice, we would not easily walk in accordance with His Word. Prophecy confirms with the Word what Jesus has spoken to us in our spirits.

I say all that to say this. When I go to visit the churches in Latin America, many times the Lord has used certain ones to give me a word of prophecy. This is a Word that confirms something to me that God has already spoken to my spirit. It also is a foretelling of events that will happen during the time I am away on a mission trip. Sometimes God has me do what is called a prophetic act to confirm something that is done in the spiritual realm. Examples of prophetic acts are seen throughout the Bible. God still does these things today as well as speak prophetically to the believers. If a person does not realize how God is doing things today according to the prophecy that went forth so many years ago, then there will be misunderstanding, judgment and confusion. This is why it is so important to have revelation of the Word as it pertains to our day and generation. God has not changed and He is still building His Kingdom in the earth today. It is a spiritual Kingdom that must be spiritually seen in the hearts of men and women.

Let me explain with one example of how God did these prophetic words and acts. A very prophetic minister of God prophesied to me just before I left to go to Peru. She said that I would be like an Esther from the Bible who would be there for such a time as that. I would come before authorities and God would tell me what to say. I would have to totally depend on him and in the right moment, He would use me to disarm the situation and bring reconciliation and peace vindicating the ones accused of wrongdoing. Now, this had never happened to me before in any of the many trips I had made to Latin America. This was a word that would cause me to be very attentive and sensitive to the voice of the Lord. I knew that if God gave that Word, then He would fulfill the Word in His way and timing.

My husband and I were together on the trip to Peru and the first day that we got to Iquitos in the jungle, we were invited to stay with a person who had recently come from the United States and was attending the church where I ministered. We moved from our hotel to his house at the request of the man from the United States, and in agreement with the Pastor I was working with. Immediately I felt in my spirit that something was wrong. I was to see how wrong things were.

Hours after we moved in, we moved back to the hotel. The man was no longer in good standing with the pastor of the church due to a recent development between them. To make a long story short, there was a language barrier because the person from the United States did not speak any Spanish and had hired an interpreter who had a devious motive about him. He was not a Christian and was twisting things according to his devices. The pastor of the church in Iquitos had entered into an agreement with this man from the United States and through misunderstanding and twisting of intentions, the pastor was held accountable for

110

mishandling things. This pastor was also being used by God to teach a lesson through all this trouble. He also learned a lesson through going through this trouble. The situation became serious and we were sort of in the middle of it like Esther was. I knew this was exactly the place that God wanted us to be in. Without the Word I had been given, I might have thought and done something to defend the pastor. But, God told me to wait until He directed me. I prayed and yielded to the Lord so I would not interfere with what He was doing. I really did feel like an Esther and I just had to trust God completely.

Some of the police in the jungle may be on the side of the Americans for whatever reason, possibly money. This had happened before and was the case. Money speaks very loudly to people who are very poor. Even good jobs do not pay much so opportunities must be handled carefully to make the most out of every opportunity. When the law is involved, bad can and did turn to worse. The situation brought the pastor and some from his family plus myself to the police station. Accusations were made, the media, of course, was summoned, and statements were signed and finger prints taken. I refused to let fear enter into my mind because I knew that it was all part of what had been prophesied to me in Florida. As I was interviewed by the TV station, I had to answer questions about why the man was wanting this pastor behind bars. The Lord moved on me as I answered and I apologized for a fellow citizen of the United States behaving in such a rude manner. I knew that because both of us were from the United States, the media expected me to defend him. I did not defend anyone, but just apologized for the display of unethical behavior that the man had exhibited. That was that and we went back to our hotel.

This man from the United States was looking for a way to publicly disgrace this pastor and destroy the ministry. He really did remind me of Haman in the book of Esther in the Bible. I knew that God would get the last word just like He did in Esther's dilemma. This man kept criticizing the pastor to his children and to me. This too was God's plan as I found out later. The man did not think that I would stay as long as I did in Iquitos and after not seeing anything of me, he had the pastor brought to the police station again to settle the matter thinking his newly acquired accusations would put him in jail. When I showed up with the pastor, he was very shocked. The influence I had as an American carried a lot of weight also. The anointing on me, my respect for the law and my integrity gave me favor before the authorities. I was asked to make a statement as a witness to this man who was defaming the character of the pastor to destroy his ministry. As I did so, it cancelled out the accusations of the man bringing the charges. The case was dismissed and God got the glory. I prayed for the man who was used by the devil to try to destroy God's people. I felt in my spirit that God would vindicate the pastor and bring judgment on this man.

When God places us in strategic positions at just the right time, we must understand that what we see is not necessarily what is really happening. Most times it goes much deeper than the surface issues. I know that that prophetic word to me in Florida from ministers from Texas who happened to be in the church I attended on the Sunday before I left for Peru was not coincidental. God had it all planned out before the world was formed. Space does not permit me to tell you all the details of this story, but rest assured, God was certainly doing awesome things in the hearts of people through it all. He had already walked through my future and had ordained it all to happen for such a time as this. He causes our faith to rise to a new level through all these things. You ask me, what became of the man who was trying to destroy the work in Iquitos? The next year when I returned, I found out that he had an accident on his motorcycle and had to return to the states. He also was involved with women and into drugs. He destroyed himself and God prospered the church and the ministry that I work with.

Satan will use whomever he will to destroy and kill the work of God. We must not be ignorant of his devices. The Bible says he roams about as a roaring lion waiting to devour someone. The ambassadors of Christ must be alert and in tune with the Spirit of the Lord to handle each situation with wisdom. The

Kingdom, the ministry, and the people of God depend on it. God is building His Kingdom and those natural examples in Scripture become spiritual examples in our lives if we understand how the spiritual realm works. His lies are not to be feared, but destroyed by the light of the gospel of truth. There is a spiritual enemy of our soul.

Chapter 11

Changing The Atmosphere

ERRORIST ACTIVITY ALSO IS A VERY PRESENT THREAT in the jungle. Iquitos is a city strategically surrounded by three major rivers. It has the Amazon River that runs all the way through Brazil to the Atlantic Ocean thus making it a critical shipping route for exports and imports. Ecuador and Peru have their differences and have had through the years. Ecuador claims that Peru has taken part of their country and they want it back so the battles begin here and there and now and then. The jungle borders both countries so Iquitos is a valuable desired conquest. It is a large city and has many lights which makes it an easy target by air if it were to be bombed.

One night I was preaching in a church in the city and suddenly the lights all went off in the city. It was pitch black out and, I mean, you could see nothing. We began to pray that God would protect the city and us and trusted the situation to him. I continued to preach in the dark and the people continued to listen. Soon someone had a candle or two and so we got some light. They did not want the lights to shine so that the city would be vulnerable to attack so the lights were off all night. We had a good service and went back to our hotel where I stayed with the pastor's wife during our time in the city. Outside of our hotel window in the street below I could hear the screams of women being raped and much crime being carried out. It was an awful situation, yet we were safe. We prayed that God would intervene in people's lives who thought only of themselves and lived for the devil. Under the cover of darkness the enemy stalks his prey. He uses the ones whose lives have been ravaged by drugs and alcohol, abuse and sin. So many people who need the Lord to transform their lives live all over the world, but right outside our window sin was rampant that night. The enemy actually is not the terrorists or those who harm other people. The enemy is sin.

It is the sin nature of human beings to destroy others just like the devil would do. Jesus is the answer and we must be a light in the world so that sin is exposed and people come to know the truth that will set them free and give them a purpose to live for. If we live for Jesus, then we will do the works of Jesus in love and the world will change. It takes people who would be willing to reach the lost and depraved with Jesus' love. It was His love for us that caused Jesus to come and give His life assuring us of eternity with Him in heaven. He does not want that any be lost. Who will tell them that Jesus loves them and has a better way to have their needs met? This is why I am there and God will let me be a light that shines into this darkness. They must see that Jesus can change them and make them whole again.

On another trip to Iquitos, I saw the bombed out shells of five buildings hit the day before by the terrorists. There were burned out buildings right in the heart of the city. Even the building that housed all the school records and such was destroyed. People who had attended the schools had to have their own records of what they had acquired to prove where they were in the education process. Systems are not as modern in these third world countries as they are where we live. Devastation is a total loss in many cases and cannot ever be restored like it once was. Banks were burned, hotels and other buildings also. This brings fear to the hearts of the people. What will give them peace in their hearts and let them sleep at night? You are right! A relationship with the Jesus that is their peace is what they need. I must go to them and I must tell them in whom this peace is found. In the midst of terrorism is the peace of God. This is the peace that passes all understanding. Psalm 23 says that God even prepares a table for us in the midst of our enemies. We can go on living in peace when we know Jesus as the Prince of Peace. This peace the world cannot give us. It is found only in Him.

There is a little café in Iquitos that seems to draw many tourists to its tables. I always go to this place because it has good food and interesting people. The waitresses are friendly, but many of them throw themselves at the men from other counties and fall into sin with them for a few extra dollars. The place has a bad reputation to some, but to me it was a place that needed the light of God. It was that very café that one little waitress saw something in me and asked questions about why I was in Iquitos. She had worked there for a few years and remembered seeing me before when I was there. I told her that I was a missionary and what I was doing with the church where I ministered. I knew that she was tired of her lifestyle and was looking for someone to make her fulfilled. I asked her if she knew Jesus Christ personally and she said she did not. I invited her to pray with me to receive the Holy Spirit of God by faith and become a child of the King. We prayed and that little waitress entered into a personal relationship with Jesus right there in that café. She was so excited and even her countenance changed because her heart had changed. I invited her to the church and she came and met many people there who welcomed her and helped her to feel comfortable. Her sins were forgiven and she had a fresh start on life. I had to go back to the United States the next day, but she began to grow in God and the youth of the church invited her to join their services and Bible studies. I know she told her friends in the café, because when I returned there, they too came to my table to ask questions. When the time is ripe and their hearts are ready, they too will ask for a better life. The choice is ours to let Jesus be Lord or live for self and be empty and hopelessly lost. There are so many in a place of decision and it is a time for those who love Jesus to be bold and let their light shine into the darkness.

The joy of the Lord and laughter is such a wonderful sign and God is releasing His people into new things. The Bible says in John 2 that God saved the best wine for last at the wedding at Cana of Galilee. What does that mean to us today? God is pouring out His spirit and it seems like it is like wine that has aged and has become extremely potent.

117

The Bible refers to wine in many places and spiritually this means the joy of the Holy Spirit. It is a wine that must have new wineskins to contain. The Word says in Matthew 9:17 that we cannot put new wine into old wineskins, that is to say bottles. This says that we cannot understand what God is doing in the earth today with our old way of thinking. We must have a new mentality that allows God to be and do what He wants. All the prophecy in the Bible will come to pass, but we must see with our spiritual eyes and hear with our spiritual ears to understand what is taking place. So many moves of God are misunderstood because we cannot change our thinking. Our wineskin (mentality) will not stretch because it has not been oiled by the Holy Spirit. A wineskin that is dry will crack and split and the wine will leak out. If we do not allow for stretching in our understanding, we will not move on with God into present day truth of the Word. It is revealed to us in our spirit and the spirit gives us understanding of its meaning for us today. The Word of God is relevant for our lives today only as we understand its spiritual meaning and apply it to our everyday lives.

This is why God wants to get us high on the new wine of His Spirit. He wants to teach us new revelations of the truth so that we can go on to perfection or maturity, not laying again the foundations mentioned in Hebrews 6 that were established in us. We must build on the foundation of the apostles and prophets like the Bible says in Ephesians 2:20. We must also do the Word or it becomes form with no power. James 1:22 speaks of this. The wine of the Holy Spirit is powerful and will transform lives and heal the brokenhearted. God wants us to have the joy of the Lord that it would be our strength to live the life that He has ordained us to live. It is a life of victory and freedom, full of power and anointing. It is a life that is full of signs, wonders and miracles that set the captives free to be all they were created to be. I want to drink of the wine of the Spirit and be full of the joy of the Lord. It is joy that sustains us even in our trials. We can rejoice in the midst of suffering and problems only as the wine of the Spirit fills us and focuses us on the heavenly reward. Jesus has not changed and He is rejoicing over us with joy. He wants a joyful bride, not a nagging wife. What do we think Jesus is looking for in his bride? I know that it is a mature bride that will be full of His joy and love.

When God wants to break a spirit of religion that holds us back from being released into the joy of the Lord, He does it in unique ways. I remember one time that I went into the prayer and fasting time at the church in Iquitos. I was a little late in arriving and the leader had all the people marching in a circle to do spiritual warfare against principalities and powers of darkness over the city. This day God decided to do something very humorous. He spoke to my spirit to go inside this circle instead of joining it. I entered the inside and began marching in the opposite direction. I did not even realize what God was trying to do. I had been praying for God to give me a message to share with them that day and I had not heard anything from Him. I always knew that those times when I did not have a message were the ones that He really did something surprising.

As I marched around in the opposite direction and caught the eye of each one, that person would fall to the floor and laughed uncontrollably. The leader marched on and those remaining marched with her. Eventually no one remained marching and still the leader marched on by herself until I stood right in front of her and looked her in the eye. The anointing hit her and she too fell on the floor in holy laughter. The joy of the Lord and the laughter released them that day of a religious spirit that held them bound in the trap of the usual. God wanted to break the mold of ritual and the habitual dead ways of doing things that He was not anointing. It was not business as usual that day. There was no anointing in what they were doing and it was tiresome and monotonous. No life came of it. This does not mean that this form of expressing ourselves is wrong. It is not effective if the anointing is not on it.

After a long while of God filling them with joy and laughter, we came to the time of sharing the Word. I now had a word to bring them because God showed us all through a demonstration what happens when our spirit is free to yield to the Holy Spirit and

119

His way of doing battle. The battle that day really was against a religious spirit that did not give life. Life must come forth as we pray, worship and serve the Lord. It cannot be just ritual and form. God does not want dead letter, but living Word. The Word is alive and we are alive in Him. What is of God has life and life more abundant. The anointing destroys the yoke of religion that so many of us have been bound with. I choose life and freedom, don't you?

We had a fun time that day and the comparison of the old way and the new was very able to be seen. God is doing new things in such amusing ways. He really does have a sense of humor. I believe His Kingdom is a fun, happy place. I believe the angels have fun. It is not boring to serve Jesus. Where there is life, there is fun too. Let the joy fill you and set you free. Time is wasting so rejoice. Focus on Him and not your situation. Let there be freedom in your life. Speak joy into your trial. The trial will not be so hard if you are filled with joy and the strength of God to endure. Put your trust in Him and let Him give you what you need to see victory in every trial.

> *Lord, fill us right now with renewed joy and strength. We are open vessels you can pour into and we yield ourselves completely to You. Let the well overflow that you have placed within us. Bubble up within us, Lord and give us life. We drink deeply of your well of living water that will satisfy the longing of our soul. Thank you Jesus for renewed strength. Amen.*

CHAPTER 12

Boats

S O MANY WONDERFUL EXPERIENCES happened through the years of going into Latin America and especially Peru. I could not begin to put them all down on paper., but they will forever be in my heart. The relationships that I have with the people living in Latin America are a precious commodity in my life. These people have taught me so much in their humble way that has changed my life forever. I will go on praying for them all of my days and hopefully visiting them again and again.

From the city of Iquitos in the Amazon Jungle, I traveled by launch down the river to many villages. The villages ranged from very primitive to jungle-style modern. I will explain as I go into more detail about each place along the banks of various key rivers. In order to have an understanding of how local people travel, I will describe at length the type of setting one would experience in the boat or launch. First, let me share about the biggest launches that carry anywhere from 200 to 500 people depending on how many stops are made and how many people board. Some of them have two decks and some have three. I have ridden on both. The bottom deck is usually used for the bigger animals such as cattle, horses, or pigs. In addition to the animals which are housed in pens usually located in the back by the so called kitchen, there is an assortment of fowl, monkeys, live fish sold to pet stores, turtles, dogs, and many other jungle creatures. These smaller animals are dispersed throughout the launch on every deck.

The river system is like the highway of the jungle so all the produce from the fields and fruit trees also is loaded unto the boat. Various seasons, of course, produce multitudes of products. There is a big harvest of bananas, sugar cane, chonta (palm heart), fruits of various kinds such as guava, oranges, and others. Sacks of rice also are piled to the roof leaving only a narrow aisle to walk through. The bathroom and shower are in the back of the boat and all pass through the sacks of rice, produce and animals to get to it.

Some of the bathrooms do not have a latch on the door so I have to rig something up with string to hold the door shut. It usually breaks in a short time as others also use it to give them some privacy. Privacy is just about non-existent in the jungle. The boats would have a bathroom, but each was a little different from the other. A normal bathroom would consist of a big plastic barrel of river water filled from time to time by the boat crew when they were not busy doing something else, a toilet without a lid or seat and maybe a shower that drew water up from the dirty river. All this is in a very small room. Some toilets do not flush and the whole population on the boat uses them. It is nasty to say the least! Once in a while someone would pour a pail of water into the toilet to wash down the contents. Do you get the picture? Need I go further? Enough said!

River water serves for everything, even to cook with. Of course, it is boiled to take out some of the impurities. There sometimes is a sink or two on the very back upper deck where people could wash their hands and face and brush their teeth if they have a toothbrush. All is river water pulled up with a pump to the sinks. I carry some hand sanitizing lotion with me and also baby wipes to cleanse myself from time to time.

The boats travel for days on the river picking up cargo and people. Some trips I took were hours long, and some days long. All the while I did not shower or usually change clothes. The privacy that the bathroom afforded was the only place to change. The floor was always full of dirty water because the shower was not separate. If there is no shower nozzle, then there is a gourd to pour water over oneself from the barrel. The boats have a little room where food is prepared over a fire and a counter that is made of wood. I will not tell you how filthy this place is. Think the worst, and then know it is worse than that! This "kitchen" usually is next to the animals. Sometimes, I rent a small room with a filthy bunk bed or two in it. Much of the baggage we carry can be kept safe in this place because we could lock it from inside and from outside with a key. Each trip I went on I usually took anywhere from five to fifteen people with me to a conference in some village. Most could not afford to travel outside the city and some were afraid of the primitive conditions and dangers. I would buy food supplies from the city for the conference and sometimes we carried bottled water with us. We used it until it was exhausted. Sometimes there were wells where we went and other times we just boiled river water for our cooking. Cleanliness was not a reality in these primitive conditions and these trips certainly would not be for those with queasy stomachs. The mind must not dwell on what could be resident in the food or on the utensils. Western culture would find it very hard to adapt to the conditions and customs.

The temperature in the jungle is probably never below 80 degrees Fahrenheit. Usually it is over 100 degrees with almost 100 percent humidity. I never quit perspiring even with a shower taken in a house or hotel. Like I said before, the seasons are hot and hotter! The insects are the worst malady that I deal with in the jungle. I can endure most anything, but I hate to itch. I never quit itching from the time I arrive in the jungle to when I leave. Sometimes I would still have bites that itched after arriving back in the states. There is one insect called a sancudo that drove me bonkers. When the insects bite in the jungle it is not a small thing. The bites swell up and get infected to some degree with pus. They last two to three weeks with reoccurring bouts with itching. The mosquitoes carry malaria and so repellent is totally necessary. The repellent does not work too well against most of the insects there and when I use it on my skin with the heat, I sometimes have a rash to contend with. I am always so "clammy" from the heat and humidity. I think I have an aroma that the mosquitoes cannot refuse!! The blood of Jesus protects me from the little pests. Many jungle diseases are in epidemic proportions in various places. Some rivers carry infestations of certain diseases more than others. If there is an epidemic in the village, sometimes there is a big sign put on the riverbank giving a warning to stay away.

In all the trips I have made to the jungle, not once have I taken any pills protecting me. By the world's thinking, I am foolish. I tried to take malaria pills once. I decided to buy some and I could not bring myself to put them in my mouth. As I put the pill to my lips, God spoke in a very clear spiritual voice to me saying, don't you trust me to protect you where I send you? I knew I would be disobedient if I took the pills so I gave them away to the pastors there. There was much malaria where I ministered and I prayed for men, women and children in the throes of the disease. Many die because there is no medicine for them in the villages where no doctor comes. They could not afford the pills if there was a doctor there to help them. Never once did I ever get sick or even have a problem with my health there. I knew God was the one who would get me through since He sent me to these people at that time. I always made sure that I only went where and when He directed. I had much confirmation in my spirit that the trip was in the perfect will of God and in His perfect timing also. Foolishness to me is getting ahead of God or doing something out of fear. I had no fear of anything, but I used wisdom and listened to the voice of the spirit. One must discern many things to risk his life where there is no medical help. This jungle is not for the faint-hearted, but for those who are sent and equipped by the Lord. This was the calling that God had placed on my life and He also equipped me and graced me to do the work without any complications.

Of course, He wants me to walk by faith and trust Him in everything I do even in the far corners of the earth. The people who live in the jungle never will have the medical facilities that we often take for granted. They must be taught the Word of God so that they can know the miracle working power of God. Faith always seems to work better when there are no options!

When a person wants to travel down the river on one of

those launches, he must go to the main port and carry all his cargo with him. This port is very, and I mean very, dangerous. I have to always keep watch over everything I bring. I take a group with me and we all have to stand guard over the things we are carrying to the conference in the river village. Much robbery and crime thrives at that port. The boats all have names and the pastor of the church in Iquitos knows which boat is going where and which one would be the best to travel on. Since I am providing the passages and the supplies, there is money to take a good boat. When I say good boat, I mean a company that is known for promptness and better facilities. To me if I have a little cabin to store our cargo, I am happy. I know things will be safe and no one can steal anything, One can never be sure what will happen on any given boat trip. So many elements are involved. The boats are all boarded by a narrow wooden plank that has slats across it for better traction and safety. It is very hard to walk up or down a plank that is only a couple of feet wide while carrying cargo. The boat is full of many different kinds of cargo. I have even seen a beat up pickup on board the prow of the boat. Often huge oil barrels are aboard going to or from the oil rigs working in the rivers. There is much oil refining and also gold refining in those rivers. There are also some Americans working in these areas with oil companies from the United States and other countries.

The boats have only one narrow board along each side. This is for passengers to sit on. Most of the passengers bring hammocks and this will be their bed and living quarters on the boat for the whole trip. By the time one day has passed and the boat has picked up people and cargo at every village, there is hardly any space to put another thing. But, just when I think they should stop picking up people and cargo, they load more. Soon the conditions have deteriorated to the point that there is no room to stand, walk or sit. Only in my hammock do I have my own space. The person next to me may have been someone from the church when we started the trip, but so many hammocks have been squeezed in between us that we are separated by unknown jungle travelers. Hammocks are hung up high, down low and at every level to get

125

more in. The boat is dangerously loaded and even listing to the side in some cases. This is because there is no room to cross over to hang their hammock on the other side because of the cargo, people and animals. All over the floor are chickens and ducks with feet tied together. There are monkeys on long ropes jumping up on the hammocks and being mischievous, taking things that don't belong to them. Underneath the hammocks that are not hung really low, are families with small children and babies. The babies do not wear diapers usually so when daylight comes, I see there is a big, smelly mess on the floor. They are too poor to even own a hammock and a tattered blanket is all they have. Sometimes I carry blankets with me to the jungle. There is a wonderful lady in North Dakota who always makes and sends some with me. This situation, of course, merits a blanket. Such is the lifestyle of those who travel on the boats in the Amazon Jungle.

I buy a new hammock for myself (a very long one) and some of the people that go with me each year I am there. A hammock does not last too many trips, but is a necessity as far as I am concerned. When the boat is very full and the things people have carried unto the boat are everywhere, it is almost impossible to even get to the bathroom. Many times there is one crawling through area to get downstairs. I literally have to crawl on my hands and knees under all the hammocks and over people and "stuff" to get downstairs. This, of course, has to be done with a flashlight in the night when all is dark. When the boat stops at each village all day long and all night long, the crawling area changes because more is brought aboard. Like I said before, imagine the worst and then know it is worse than that.

By now you may ask how I cope with all this and keep my attitude right. It is the grace of God and the calling that I have that just lets me endure most everything with no problems. Actually, I consider it an honor to be able to be with these people who need the love of the Lord so much. It is an awesome responsibility to represent Jesus Christ to these people. It also is an awesome responsibility to represent the United States. I may be the only Christian they see or even the only American for that matter. I want people to think of my God and my country with love and gratitude. When they hear me talking Spanish and realize that we can communicate, they have hundreds of questions for me. I love to speak Spanish and tell them of Jesus and also about the United States. I speak highly of both and tell them we pray for them there in the jungle. I also love to ask them questions about their life in the jungle. I am fascinated with how primitive people cope with their environment and how they use what they hunt, fish and grow to live from. Some business is done without money, just trading one thing needed for another needed thing. It works and has for centuries. The people that I have met have been wonderful to me and I appreciate their friendship very much. Most of them I will never see again, but the ones who invite Jesus to be Lord of their lives I will see again in heaven.

This is the life on a boat trip. Each trip is different and unique, but the bottom line is that all of us need one another. Sometimes I bring balloons and candy for the kids on the boat. Boy, am I a favorite after that! I know how to make balloons into animals and swords, etc. and it passes the time for the kids as they watch and want to learn. I leave some balloons and my balloon pump with someone whom I teach to make the balloons into animals and shapes. The modern contraptions that come from the United States are something seen for the first time by these people. They don't have a clue what goes on in other parts of the world. They have only seen the world through one perspective. Once in a while I may see a black and white TV that gets one or two channels in a village that has a generator and electricity some of the time. Some may get to see the news from the country of Peru and possibly other parts of the world. Electricity usually is available from a generator on the weekend evenings for a couple of hours. It is very expensive to run the generators so sometimes they just sit idle because of lack of money from the government.

The boats have some inadequate life vests aboard, but they hang on the rafters and it would be utter chaos if there actually were a need for them. The sides of the boats have plastic tarp on them to protect the people from the rainstorms. The Amazon

River is so incredibly big that it is like being on the ocean to me. It is the largest river in the world or at least the second largest depending on whom you talk to. It is a dirty brown river because of the riverbanks falling into it. The river has a current that is so strong that when it enters the Atlantic Ocean in Brazil, it is visible from the air for over five miles. When I bathe in the river, I have to hang on to the shore digging my fingers into the mud to keep from being dragged down stream. There are huge whirlpools in the river which are very dangerous. As storms arise, the boat is in great peril because of the oversized load of people and cargo and because of the waves. Many boats have sunk beneath the waters of the Amazon River in years past. Phantom boats appear on the water at times because of the witchcraft and voodoo that is so prevalent in the jungle. This is a visible phenomenon something like the ghosts and apparitions that haunt castles and houses. There are so many people who have lost their lives because of boat and canoe accidents that the familiar spirits of these people are demonically active. We will talk about witchcraft a little later in the book. It is a very real religion in the jungle.

Once when I was riding down the river with some pastors from the city and some of the villages, I realized that the captain of the boat was only a teenager or maybe in his early twenties. The pastor's wife told me that sometimes the competition between boat companies is so strong that the younger pilots try to play "chicken" with the boats. In the middle of the night I was awakened from my sleep feeling like something was wrong. The pastor's wife was awake too and we saw two big boats coming closer and closer. The one we were riding on belonged to the government and seemed to have the upper hand so to speak. Here we were in the middle of this "game of chicken" with nothing we could do except pray, which we did. The boats were going full speed against the current in the middle of the river coming so close to each other that we could almost shake hands with the people on the other boat. Both boats challenged each other for several minutes and all of a sudden they crashed together. People were sleeping in their hammocks on both boats and very few people saw what happened. We saw it all and knew that God protected everyone because of prayer and intervention of his angels. There were loud screams as we crashed into each other and all were awake wondering what happened. I found out that this happens more often than one would like to think. The boat we were on "won" and we continued down the middle of the river while the other boat went way over to the other side. The immaturity of these boat pilots risking everyone's life just to satisfy their egos, made many people outraged and I am sure the owner heard about it when the boat returned. I do not know if anyone cared or not that this sort of incident happens from time to time. I will never know. The law of the jungle is very different than the law in the United States. The life is wild and full of surprises and I had to learn to roll with the punches. I am so glad that I have a God who watches over me and intercessors in the United States who pray faithfully for my safety. Without people joined with me in intercession, I would have had many calamities as the enemy of the gospel tried to stop the Word from setting people free from demonic strongholds. The jungle is a place where a person must learn to pray without ceasing because of the dangers and the conditions.

There were some storms on the river that blew into the boat with such great velocity that all the hammocks, cargo and floors were totally soaked with water. The hammocks did not dry fast and we had to sleep in them wet. There was nothing else to be done. The plastic tarp usually was in very bad condition and did not hold out wind or rain very well. Storms could come up in the night without warning as squalls passed along the river. There was nowhere to take cover so we had to endure it. I thought of Paul in the book of Acts in the Bible and what he endured in the storms on the sea. God took care of him and He takes care of me too. I just consider it all an adventure in the Amazon Jungle and journal it in my notebook. I know God does not want me to be disappointed because of lack of excitement so He always provides me with plenty. I just trust Him and enjoy the ride.

As the boat goes deeper into the jungle, the rivers join with

129

other large rivers and the water changes color accordingly. The Amazon is always the dirtiest and the most dangerous. There are two seasons of heavy rains in the jungle and all the rivers flood over their banks even into the houses in some places. The huts are built along the riverbanks on stilts because of these floods. If the floods are too high, the people have to move out of their houses for a season until the waters abate. They sleep in hammocks in the huts too so there is not much that can get destroyed. All is made of wood with plenty of space between the small boards to let the water drain through.

Many times I have seen pink dolphins jumping and playing in the rivers. I thought that they were just a legend, but there are hundreds of dolphins visible as the boat goes down river. There are also small alligators and huge anacondas and boas in the waters. The most deadly creatures are the piranhas that come in all different sizes. These fish are flesh eaters and will devour a whole cow in minutes in a feeding frenzy. Needless to say, people do not do much swimming in the river except close to shore. The river serves as the bathing place, the bathroom and the food supply plus it is the highway for all traffic. In numerous villages there are no bathrooms of any kind nor is there a place to bathe. There is absolutely no privacy anywhere. I take a small dome-shaped tent to sleep in and that gives me a covering to change clothes and sleep. Without my tent, I would be really vulnerable. God is good and all goes well as I stay in the villages and ride on the boats. Like I said, it is certainly an exciting adventure to me and I love it. The heat is excruciating, but I learn to live with these temperatures also. I live in Florida now so the climate is not as difficult for me to endure. When I lived in North Dakota and left the severity of the winter there to go to the extreme heat in the jungle, that was a big change!

The river has many dangers like I stated before. One very real threat is the terrorist activity. The large launches are prey to river pirates who use speedboats to overtake them and then board with firearms and rob the people. This is so devastating especially when they have just transported all their products to market and are returning with a small amount of money for their whole year's existence. These pirates are very busy in the deepness of the jungle where the river is completely dark except for the moonlight. Very few villages are visible from the riverbanks and it is a sure setup for tragedy. There is not police control, of course, and the people are at the mercy of these robbers. I feel so badly for these poor people when this happens. I have never been robbed on any trip I have gone on down these rivers. I have been robbed though in the port while waiting for the boat to depart.

Wisdom comes quickly when lessons are learned through ignorance. I pay close attention now to everybody and everything that is going on around me. I fell victim to a little scheme that is often used for a distraction and opportunity to steal. I carry all my precious possessions in a backpack that I always keep in my hand. This particular backpack held my most valued bilingual Bible, my notes to preach from, my cameras and tape recorder, my glasses, sweater, and numerous other smaller items. I do not carry my passport, money or non-replaceable items in my backpack. These ports always have hundreds of workers selling just about anything one could ever have need of on a riverboat trip. They board the boats and sell things right up to departure time. The boats are full of passengers, people delivering cargo, and those who sell things. We had just boarded and the first item of business was to find a good spot to put the hammock so we could be together as a group. We always tried to get close to the front so there was a wall on one side and the chance of getting split up by others putting hammocks in between ours was less. The pastor's son was carrying all the food and materials we were taking along unto the boat. He took my backpack and placed it in the hammock next to me so no one would occupy it. I was keeping my hand on it even though it was in the next hammock. Two young men came over to me to sell me some apples that looked interesting. I thought they might be good to nibble on during the trip so I was in the process of digging some money out of my pocket to pay for them. As the one young man was handing me the apples, the other young man moved over to the side of the boat, grabbed my backpack and flung it over the side to a partner in crime down below on the shore. He immediately took off with it. The pastor's son who put it there was just arriving with another load of cargo and I told him what had just happened. He took off like a rocket and tried to follow this young man with the backpack. The other two escaped in the crowd of people, but I remember what they looked like. It did not matter, nothing would ever be done about it because it happened all the time and everyone just had to take chances to ride the boats. The pastor's son could not find him because he probably had a motorcycle or something to get away fast. He spread the news to some people working at the port and gave them a description of the backpack that was probably one of a kind there. He promised them I would pay fifty dollars to anyone who would bring me the backpack with the contents inside and at least something if some of the contents were there. Fifty dollars is more than some people earn in six months so it was incentive I'll tell you! I never saw my backpack again. As I waited on the boat with the rest of the group with me, the pastor's son returned and felt so bad for putting my backpack in that hammock to reserve it. He asked me if I wanted to call off the trip thinking I had lost documents and much money that was needed for the trip.

Do you know what happened? Tremendous joy rose up in my spirit and I began to laugh and rejoice. This was not something I could do in the natural. It was a supernatural release of the joy of the Lord that was in me for such a time as this. Now I surprised everyone of course! I just understood that even in trials there could be exceeding joy and freedom. The Word of God was truly manifested that very moment and it spread to all the others. People were watching us with unbelief that I could have such joy when I had just been robbed. It was really not something I understood, but I knew God was doing something through it all to work good out of evil.

You see, God revealed to me in my spirit that He wanted to reach that young robber for the Kingdom and the way He chose to do it was to have him steal my backpack. The treasure in the backpack was not what he was looking for, but the treasure that

God wanted him to have was in that backpack. It was the Bible which was both in English and in Spanish. Also the tape that was in the tape player was a revelation hot off the press that morning. I had just preached in the church a wonderful message of Jesus' love and His plan for our lives to get us to our destiny in Him. It was preached in Spanish so he could even understand it. The joy came because of what God showed me. He would realize that he had robbed a pastor or a missionary and God would surely bring him to justice. God's justice many times is his mercy and grace. I believe that this young man was about to have his life turned around because of having that Bible and that message. There are no coincidences with God. He has a way that is above our ways. When I shared what God had shown me, they could understand why it all happened as it did.

Days later when I arrived at the village where I would do the conference, the joy was still full in me. I would laugh as I began to prepare my message without my Bible or my notes. Would you believe that the village did not have any electricity and I had to preach by candlelight. I could not have even seen to read the Bible if I had one. Hardly anyone of the people at the conference had a Bible because they had no money or chance to go to the city where they were sold. I did not have the Bible in paper, but the Word was hidden in my heart and I preached using the Word that God quickened in my spirit. The meetings were filled with joy and release as I related what happened on the boat. We all learned that joy does not depend on circumstances, but on the life of Jesus within. If the world did not give us that joy, then the world cannot take it away. Jesus is the joy in my heart and Jesus will change the atmosphere if I will focus on Him. Joy must be demonstrated. It is a fruit of the Spirit and the Bible says, by our fruits we will be known whether we be of God or not. Everything must be tested, but Jesus knows that His grace is sufficient in time of need. I was blessed by this whole ordeal and so were all the others. Jesus certainly won the day and the devil suffered a big defeat. What the devil sent to discourage me, God turned around for His glory and lives were forever changed. I must not ever look at things in the natural realm that I see because God is doing something much deeper and more important in the spiritual realm that I can't see. It is a joy to serve the Lord who is always teaching me and giving me wonderful learning adventures.

Many of my trips to the jungle find the Amazon River in a low stage, which is not as dangerous. When the boats dock at the riverbanks to load people and cargo, they have an easier time of it because the banks are visible. When there is flooding, the boat may not be able to get close enough to shore to load or unload. It is very difficult to bathe in the river because the current is stronger than usual and I do not know where the water drops off into the deep. There are more whirlpools when the river has grown. The natives travel in small canoes on the river and some have been caught in the whirlpools and pulled under because they could not escape and went round and round until they drowned. I have a lady pastor friend that told me stories of her trips across the river to meetings at night. With only the light of the moon, she would navigate across the river and at times she got in trouble with the whirlpools. Many times she was protected by God when she thought she could not escape the circular pulls she was in. All of a sudden the canoe came out of the whirlpool and she knew that it was only that God had answered her prayer. God had a plan for her life and she was a brave, adventurous pastor to cross that river alone at night. I saw something in her that was also in me. The people must be reached at any cost. She started several churches in the jungle villages and was a powerful apostle over those churches. We did conferences in her village from time to time.

One time when the river was flooding, a group of pastors from a nearby village came to pick me up at a port where the boats passed and picked up passengers. A small group of pastors from the city were with me. We had to travel into a lagoon and then through the jungle proper. The river did not flow in a straight line, but made many "hairpin" turns as it wound through the jungle. When the river flooded, it was possible to just cross over the flooded land through the dense jungle growth thus saving much time and effort. I was so thrilled and fascinated at the beauty

134

going under the trees. These lagoons provided many of the tropical species of fish that are sold to pet stores in the United States. The fishing was very good and provided fish for them to eat. I had to watch carefully as we went under the trees. Big snakes and poisonous snakes flourish in this jungle. Also the tree branches were right in our faces so we had to push them aside and maneuver through the dense growth of trees finding a channel that was wide enough to pass through. This was my kind of trip! This canoe was a little bigger and could carry several people. Once off the Amazon River, the current became much easier to row against. We all took turns rowing because of it being so strenuous and tiring for two. The canoe had a motor, but they had no money for gas so it was not useable for the trip. I was able to buy them gas on the return trip. We found fishermen putting big catches of fish in a holding net on the side of the lagoon. We asked them if we could buy some fish to take to the village and they sold us some. We had them for dinner that night. I like the taste of the fish there, but the piranha is my favorite because it is sweet and has bigger bones. The fish is grilled over a fire and served whole. The jaws of the piranha can be kept for a souvenir. Their teeth are razor sharp and can shred most anything in minutes.

Once we got to the very small village on the other side of the loop in the river, we pitched our tents and got ready for the conference. The children were so excited to see a white person come way back to where they lived. I do not believe they had ever had a missionary come to visit them from the United States. They fished for me and presented me with two or three fish each day for my meal. They were supposed to be in school, but the teacher would stand at the door of the school and ring the bell without any of them reporting for class. I guess I was more educational at that time. I visited the school and talked with the teachers. They have hard jobs to be so remote and the pay is so bad. The children learn very slowly because of the conditions and also because the villages are so ingrown among themselves. Incest is very prevalent and it slows the mind. It takes a long time to capture the informa-

135

tion being taught. It is a sad situation that these people live in, but it has gone on for centuries and not changed.

Just about every village has some sort of a school and the teachers have classes at two or three of them a week sometimes. The government slowly is building better schools in the villages and also sidewalks in some. May I say that the best thing the government builds is the outhouse! I actually saw three outhouses in that village. There was privacy at least for me. The outhouse contained only a hole in the ground. Nothing to sit on was available. The space was very small, but it was private and I was overjoyed. It is not the most pleasant thing to talk about, but so you understand the conditions there that I must live in, I am telling you these things. The bathroom in many villages is wherever you want it to be. In other words, there are none.

It was very interesting to watch the people in these remote and primitive areas. The church had to always encourage the people to use the outhouses to keep the village more sanitary. The people were not accustomed to such conveniences and had to train themselves to adapt to change. These outhouses had just recently been put there so the process of change would take time. Each time that I return to the jungle, I do see progress. The world we live in so drastically changes as we travel to far away places. I often wonder how we can be so modern and comfortable here in the United States and so totally at the mercy of the environment in another part of the world. I know that there are probably less problems in the more primitive areas because of less to contend with. To find food to eat and to stay healthy I would say are the major issues in the remote villages.

As we teach the people the Word of God, there is a hope that comes into their lives. The superstitions and dependence on witchdoctors has to be broken so that life can be full of joy even in their traumatic environments. The head pastor in the city of Iquitos has trained, to some degree, pastors for each village where we go to do a conference. There usually is no church but the one that he has started. Some larger villages do have many small churches that have been started by missionaries who have come.

Some of these churches are Christian churches and some are not. The dependency on witchdoctors is growing less and less and the people are coming out from under the curses that have been put on them. The anointing of God destroys the yoke of bondage from demonic powers and the people are set free to believe in a God who loves them and has a plan for their lives. The truth of the Word always sets people free to be what they were created to be and to enter into fellowship with a living God who will guide them by His Holy Spirit. There are many spirits in the world, but the Holy Spirit is the Spirit of truth and He will guide people into truth. The people must see the difference between the Holy Spirit and the demonic spirits that bring curses and death. Jesus Christ came to bring life and life more abundantly to all peoples and nations and tribes. It is a joy to see their countenances change when truth sets them free from superstition and darkness in their spirit. There truly is a light that shines when Jesus comes into the hearts of those who receive Him by faith. The eyes of their understanding begin to grasp the purpose of life and the destiny prepared for them in heaven spending eternity with Jesus Christ. Everyone will spend eternity in either heaven or hell and the Word has commanded us to go into all the world and preach the gospel to the lost. This is the great commission spoken of in the Bible in Mark 16:15.

As believers redeemed by the blood of Jesus, we have a responsibility to Jesus as His ambassadors to share His love into the hearts of men, women and children even in the farthest and most remote corners of the earth. To me, this jungle is one of these corners and He has called me, equipped me, and sent me to these wonderful people. It is a privilege to live with them for a short while and share the love of Jesus with them. When they welcome me, they are welcoming the Jesus that lives in me to their village. He will reveal Himself in powerful ways to them and bless them. His love must shine forth from us so that the world can see that this Jesus is alive and building His Kingdom here on this earth in the hearts of men, women and children. As long as Jesus sends me to the jungle, I will go and do His work among the people there.

I keep my focus on the Lord and the work He wants me to do. The conditions are hard to live with, but the love in me for God and His people will always triumph over the situations I must contend with. I feel so blessed to be a part of their lives and they have given me a joy inside like no other. We are friends and we are family through the Spirit of the Lord. It is a mystery how this can be, but I know it is true. Those who have the Spirit of the Lord can relate to Christians in any walk of life in any place in the earth. We become one in the body of Christ worldwide. The language we all speak is the language of love and it is understood by each one. God wants that not one be lost and that all would come to the knowledge of the truth in Him. He is drawing all nations to Himself, yet many will turn their backs on the love that God gives and an eternity in heaven. Many will only live to kill and destroy because there is no love of Jesus in their heart.

Do you see how important it is to receive the love of God for ourselves and then share that love with others? It is more than doing things for people out of kindness. It is being one with Jesus with this love abiding in us. His love is unconditional and will pay any price. Can you say that this love dwells in you? Would you like to pray for a greater relationship with Jesus to demonstrate His love to your family, to your neighbors and even to those who hate you? In Matthew 5 in the Bible, Jesus asks us to even love our enemies. This is only done through the love that He gives. Jesus loved us so that we can love others.

Heavenly Father, I receive your love for me and I thank you for your mercy and patience with me as I learn to trust You. Help me, Lord, to love those whom You have put in my life. Cause me not to look at their shortcomings and faults, but to cover them with the love that I receive from you. Let me see people through your eyes and love them like you do. Help me to understand that love is a fruit of your Spirit abiding in me and that it is my choice to let that love flow or to hold it back. Father, I choose this day to love unconditionally. I need your grace to help me stay free from offenses and hurts. Your grace is sufficient as I yield myself to you. Thank you, Lord, for who you are. Amen

CHAPTER 13

Go With The Flow

ETTING A BOAT TO GO DOWN THE RIVER is sometimes very frustrating. If we leave from the main port in Iquitos, it is not so hard because all the boats dock there and we can choose which one to take. There are varied prices for the passages depending on how good the boat is. Sometimes we go to another port that has several boats also, but they are smaller and not very safe in the currents. Many boats have capsized in the rivers from the current and the storms. On one of my last trips on the river, the people told me of a boat that capsized the previous month and all were drowned. That was so sad and sometimes I think it may have been because of foolishness and neglect of common sense. I pray very hard when I travel those rivers.

Leaving the main port sometimes has draw backs too because the boats often malfunction and they have to turn around and we all have to carry our belongings off and wait until another one is ready. This has happened to me more than once and is frustrating to say the least. We lose many precious hours that cause the meetings I need to be at to be delayed. The people in the villages often stand waiting for me to arrive on the boat so they can help carry our belongings. Even in the middle of the night, they get up and run to the riverbank to greet me. It makes me feel so special and I appreciate their love and hospitality so much. They are thrilled that we can communicate in Spanish. I have never been to tribes that speak only Quechua dialects. These are the indigenous languages that the tribes speak. These tribes are located on the smaller and more remote rivers towards Brazil and Ecuador. The sizes of the people vary so much depending on what their origin is. I do not believe I have ever seen anyone yet, man or woman, taller than me. I am five feet ten inches tall and this is very tall for the jungle.

I have so many invitations to come back to villages I have been to before and also to very remote tribes that live so far away, it would take a long time to travel by river. Because of connections and needing a canoe at the end because of the small rivers, it could easily take weeks just going one way. There are people living in these areas that do not even wear clothes. Some may wear a skirt of pounded tree bark or of grass. I have seen both tribes that dress like this. It is a totally primitive lifestyle back along the smaller rivers. No one from the outside travels there very often if at all. There is rampant disease and also terrorism is very high because of the drug trafficking. The pastors that invite me say that men would be killed if they came back there, but a woman would be safer. I am praying about the possibility of reaching those areas some day if God sends me there. I know it would be very risky, but if God sends me, He will protect me and use me to bring liberty in the spirit to the people.

Many times when we have been in a village for a few days and want to catch a boat to return back to Iquitos after the meetings, we cannot get one to come over to pick us up. I have waited with all my belongings packed including my hammock and tent for more than a day. The boats come by during the day and night, but some just do not want to stop to pick us up or they are too full and cannot take on any more passengers. During the day the boats can see us, but at night we must use a torch or several flashlights to flag the boat over. I have actually waited in the hot sun all afternoon and into the night. I am so tired after preaching twice a day all week that I just lie down on the dirt and put a sheet over myself and sleep. The mosquitoes are so fierce that they bite me right through the sheet. We all must be at the riverbank to hear the boat coming. Time after time they pass and never stop. There can be no real time schedule along these rivers because a person will get to where he is going when he gets there! Everything is at the mercy of the boats. We waited so long for boats going to the city of

Iquitos to stop for us. None stopped for us so we boarded a boat going farther up the river just to get on one. We traveled all night and the next day and later arrived right back where we started from, but we were on the boat. It still took us two more days to get back to the city. You can imagine how dirty and sweaty we were after all that. We would be glad to be back to civilization as we knew it. Our group was about fifteen people so we had to have a boat that could take us all. Sometimes the boats do not stop at the riverbank because it is too dangerous. They send out a motor boat to pick people up and get them to the launch. This is only if there are one or two people traveling. The problem is that the current plus the flooding in the river eats away the banks made of soft brown soil. I actually watch the banks fall into the river in big chunks. The village we were in waiting for the boat had such a problem. The buildings had to be abandoned that were close to the river for fear of them falling in. The river changes some of the village embankments within a few years. The houses need to be fairly close to the river because it is what they use for bathing and for drinking and cooking. To carry heavy buckets of water a long distance is very hard and tiring. When I stayed in this village I bathed myself using a gourd and a bucket of water someone brought me. I just bathed in the house without any privacy. I bathed in my shorts and t-shirt since I had no other alternative. Being a Christian, I could not be naked out there of course! The people always watched me do everything just because I was the new kid on the block I guess. They got a kick out of how I just did it! All modesty goes in places like that and I learned to survive just fine. Pride has no place on the mission field if you have not realized that by now!

When a village is inland and I have to walk a long distance, I take a little group of pastors with me to get me there. These villages send pastors to the conference and then want me to visit their village when I am done ministering. I wear one of those vests that have oodles of pockets on them for times like this. I can load it up with my mosquito repellent, food, flashlight, antiseptic, band-aids, string, jackknife, snakebite kit, and whatever else will

141

fit. It is incredibly hot there so I really perspire with all the extra weight on me. The leader has to carry a machete to move the grass in front of her or him so the snakes do not bother us. There are some that are very deadly and kill almost instantly. I am glad to be the second in line of course and besides that, I do not know where I am going.

The jungle is so interesting as I see the wildlife. There are lots of monkeys jumping in the trees and when I look up into the trees, I see huge mounds of dirt that are either bee's nests or ant's nests. The ants are huge and edible. I have eaten the ants when they are boiled. I even have some in a display box at my home in Florida to show people so they will see how big they are. I do not think that we have any in the United States that big. The part of the ant that is eaten is the rear bulb. It is chewy and is filled with a liquid like substance. They actually were not too bad to the taste. I don't think I would like to eat many of them though. I also have eaten a caterpillar- like worm that is fried. They have a small, hard head that is not eaten. The skin is a little tough to chew and the insides are not like anything I have ever tasted. The taste is not good, but not bad either. I would eat more if I had to. I prefer my insects fried I have decided. This worm only is found on certain trees I am told. How fortunate I was to have an adventure with new and different food. The pastors laugh as I just seem to eat anything that they eat. The real test was when I was served monkey. The worst part of it is eating something we might have for a pet in this country. The meat is sinewy and tough since it is wild. The fur is singed off over the fire and the monkey cut up and boiled in a big pot. The meat is usually used to make a soup and as I sat at the table viewing each person's bowl of monkey soup, I knew that no part of the monkey was wasted. I had the ribs and I can't say that I like wild meat at all. I always say grace before I eat and remember the scripture in the Bible that nothing will harm me when God is protecting me. I have eaten animals that are from the rat family also. These animals are used similarly to how we would use a pig. They fry the meat over a fire like we would pork or bacon. This too was very tough meat.

There are several roots that are eaten and used in cooking. One of these is called yuca. It is white and is fried or it can be masticated, mixed with saliva and spit into a container. This mixture is combined with sugar cane I believe and water and some other things and used for a drink. It is called masato or chicha in jungle places. It tastes very acidic and smells terrible. It is said to have many nutrients in it for the health. Even the children drink this. The women who have the best teeth are the ones selected to do the chewing and mixing with their saliva. I have had this several times and it tells them that I am really one of them. This drink becomes fermented over time and is very potent when it is a few days old. This too is good for the digestive system they say. I have never had a problem with drinking it, but I do not drink much you understand! It really tastes terrible! It would take some getting used to if I had to live out in remote areas and have it often.

Bird eggs are eaten there as well as turtle eggs. These eggs are not the greatest in comparison to chicken eggs. I prefer to stick with chicken eggs. The turtle meat is pretty good to eat. These are river turtles that taste different from salt-water turtles. The animals are captured in many different ways. Anything high in the trees must be shot with a dart from a blowgun. These are long tubes made from small tree branches and decorated with seeds and painted with mixtures of various substances. The arrows they use are very thin and fly far. Often they are coated with a poisonous mixture that speeds up the dying process of the monkey or bird.

The most challenging part of walking inland is crossing the deep ravines that are formed by small rivers flowing to the Amazon. There is not much water in them except during flood time. A large, long tree trunk is placed from bank to bank so to make a bridge that can be walked on. A person must have pretty good balance to be able to walk across. Sometimes one must sit down and just scoot across. The whole group I was with made it by helping those behind steady themselves while walking. An outstretched arm is really handy for support. Now I understand a little better that scripture in the Bible that talks about God's outstretched arm. (Jeremiah 27:5)

On one particular hike through the interior, we had to cross the same river five times to get to the village and five times to return to join the others waiting where we did the conference. I loved the adventure of it all even when I am over fifty! God just blessed me with so many experiences like these. I am not sure the others enjoyed the trek through the interior as much as I did, but we all made it there and back without any complications. If someone would have fallen off the tree trunk and into the depth of the ravine, if could have been very serious. Any broken limbs would have definitely caused major panic. God, I know, had His outstretched arm there to steady us as we went and blessed the little village that day. I took pictures using a borrowed camera. This was the trip where my backpack was stolen so my camera was never to be seen by me again. The borrowed camera did not produce any pictures that were good. I had no record except in my memory and heart of that trip inland. The cameras do not last long in the jungle because of the humidity. I have given some with film to the pastors and within a year, they do not work. Hopefully I will get another opportunity to go into the interior and visit the villages there that are not visited often by any outside missionaries. The people are very encouraged when we make the effort to come and see them. It is not an easy trip nor is it impossible. We just must have the time and the willingness to go to these places.

I feel called to be in that jungle and live in those conditions because God had graced and equipped me to do it. If you do not have a calling for the jungle, please do not go. God will not send you where He does not equip you first. The equipment I have is a stomach that can eat almost anything without any problems and a resistance to disease and heat. Also I have a tremendous love for the primitive peoples of the world and a longing to teach them the Word of God. My happiest days have been spent in that jungle with those people doing God's work. This too is only because that was the destiny that God ordained for me to walk into. He had it all planned out and knew every step it would take to get there. When I think about how it all came to pass, I stand at awe of his goodness and grace.

Now I hope you have some idea of how people live in the place where I work. I can see things like this on TV programs doing documentaries about primitive cultures, but there is nothing like being there for me. You on the other hand, may be very happy to watch it all on TV! Isn't it wonderful how different we each are and yet there is a call to reach those who need a personal relationship with Jesus Christ wherever they are. Everyone needs to have a hope and a future in Heaven spending eternity with the true and living God who sent His son to die for our sins that we can receive Him and His finished work on the cross.

Many false gods are in the world today. Jesus warns us that deception will come and even the very elect can be deceived. We must be very discerning in these days. There is only one true God. His Word is true and all the prophecy in it is coming to pass just like He said. Jesus Christ came to this earth and gave his life for our salvation. He shed His blood for the remission of our sins. He was resurrected and is sitting at the right hand of the Father in heaven. He sent His Holy Spirit to convict of us sin and to transform us from the kingdom of darkness to His Kingdom of light. By receiving the Holy Spirit by faith into our hearts, we can be saved and part of the family of God. We must believe that He exists and that He lives in the hearts and lives of people on this earth who will receive His sacrifice for their sin. He is holy and without sin. He was tempted like we are, yet He did not sin. His character is pure and righteous. He is the only way to be saved. He says in His Word that He is the Way, the Truth and the Life and no one can come to the Father except by the blood of Jesus Christ as a sacrifice for their sin. He has bridged the gap between the sin of Adam whereby all were born into sin and our eternity in Heaven with Him. Will we understand the importance of this sinless sacrifice for humanity? God had a plan for us from the beginning. No one can improve on what He has done. Though many try and claim to be the savior of the world, only Jesus will be able to cleanse us from sin. His blood has the power to cleanse, heal and deliver us from the life of self. I lay my life down that His life may dwell in me. I will do what He has asked of me and because of my love for Him and His people, it will be a pleasure and a joy to serve Him. I pray that you will desire a relationship with Jesus if you do not have one. There is nothing on this earth that can satisfy like Jesus. We have only so many allotted days on this earth and then it is over. If we surrender to Jesus and receive Him makes all the difference for eternity.

Lord Jesus, I am tired of going my own way and doing my own thing. I want to surrender my life to You, so that I can be free from a desire to sin. I repent of my sins and I ask You to forgive me, cleanse me, and set me free from sin. I believe in my heart You are the Son of God who died for my sins. I yield my will to yours and gladly receive this precious gift of salvation. I invite you to fill me with your Holy Spirit. Thank you, Lord, for your love for me. In Jesus' name I pray. Amen.

CHAPTER 14

Villages

ONE OF MY FAVORITE VILLAGES to go to on the Amazon River is a little place about eight hours from Iquitos. This village has a church and a pastor who is a powerful woman of God. The village has a new school now and also a clinic that has a medic visit every so many months. There were no bathrooms the last time I was there, but there is a lot of open space! The river is close to the pastor's house and I pitch my tent in her house or in the church when I visit. The river is my bathtub, water supply and anything else I need. It usually is not in flood mode when I go, but one year it was. It just makes it a lot more inconvenient and dangerous when it is flooding over the banks. There is a hill in the village that has a path that follows the river for a ways. There are only two paths through the village that is long and narrow. There are paths out the inland side of the village that go into the interior to other small villages. The houses are made of split, small tree trunks and the roof is woven palm leaves. The floors are usually boards placed far enough apart to let dirt and water through. The house consists of one or two rooms and placed on stilts because of the flooding. Animals run in and out of the houses at will. There are not really dangerous large animals around although tigers live in the mountains. The people use animal skins to cover their drums. The drums are usually tall and have a good sound. I have even seen six year olds play the drum with perfect rhythm. The kids are very musically inclined as most of the people there are.

The village has had terrorists come and threaten to kill some of them if demands were not met. The pastor there told me of one incident where a terrorist put a gun in her mouth ready to kill her when one of the terrorists recognized her from somewhere and told the man not to kill her. What a close call and we all know that God intervened and changed their hearts that day. He does protect his ministers or none of us would be alive going through some of the situations that arise. I know that my life has been spared several times. The terrorist threats rise and fall depending on the organization of the groups. The groups are caught from time to time and put in jail or worse and a new leader must take over. I have seen some terrorism, but nothing like there used to be a few decades back.

In this little village where there was only electricity a couple of hours on the weekend, a wonderful thing happened especially among the children. They would be up at the crack of dawn and go into the one little church that was there. All through the village would be heard the sounds of the children singing and playing the drum and tambourine. There was such joy in their hearts that they loved to get together and praise the Lord whenever they could. Many of their parents were not even believers, yet the children were sensitive to the Lord. A child shall lead them says the Word. It was a beautiful sight to see and I loved to hear them sing as I was waking up each morning.

We had wonderful times in the services in the church with pastors from neighboring villages walking hours through the jungle at night with small children to get there. The people were spiritually hungry to be taught the Word of God and worship the Lord together. A conference was a special time, and none of the pastors wanted to miss it. Some would arrive in canoes loaded dangerously full with too many people. I always brought plenty of flashlights with me to give to the pastors. They knew the jungle and rivers so well that all they traveled by was the light of the moon. It was so dangerous, yet their love for God and the gathering of the people was greater. It blessed my heart and made me think about how spoiled we are in the United States. We have so much, but we lack the zeal for God and the hunger for the Word. Many of us make so many excuses why we cannot go to church.

When I saw what they went through to get to those services, it made me very convicted about my own dedication and commitment to church. I have always been faithful, but sometimes I get apathetic and just take church for granted. Life has a way to get into a rut very easily. These people taught me a lot about what was important in life as a Christian. I could make a lot of changes in my attitudes, I felt, and I know that God looks on the heart motivations. Those that are humble and poor may be richer than we are in the God's economy.

One beautiful day, we decided to have the first March for Jesus in that village. We shared with the people what we were going to do and then gathered at the church to walk through the village. We carried and played the instruments as we marched and sang praises to God. The people came out from their houses to see what was happening and we told them that Jesus loved them and they could know Him personally as Lord and Savior. The gospel was shared and many joined our ranks as we continued to march to the end of the village and back again. When we were finished, a big, beautiful rainbow filled the sky. I sensed that God was very pleased that day because He was glorified in the eyes of the people. The Bible says if He is exalted He will draw all people unto Himself. (John 12:32) The service in the church that night had many new believers come from the village. This was a day of evangelism. Even with only one church in the village, many people did not come because of their superstitions and witchcraft.

Witch doctors live in the village too, and one night when I was preaching, suddenly I began to cough and I felt I was dying because I could not breathe. I recognized that a man had walked in the back of the church and was putting a curse on me. The curse was very strong and a spirit of death was associated with it. Voodoo is real, but the Name of Jesus spoken by the authority of the believer has greater power to break the curse. This is because the blood that Jesus shed at the cross has power to defeat the demonic realm. It is not a game, and one must not speak without the authority of heaven behind the words. The whole jungle has had centuries of witchdoctors and satanic influences. The light of

149

the gospel shines into the hearts of mankind with the truth of who Jesus Christ is. This earth belongs to God because He created it and rules and reigns over it. The devil is defeated, but He and his spiritual hoards still roam in the earth seeking their prey. He preys on the ignorance of people who have not heard the truth of the Word. The struggle between good and evil has gone on since the Garden of Eden. It will continue until Jesus returns to earth to take the believers that remain on this earth to heaven. It is all written in the Bible. The Bible is the truth and it is the way we stay informed of what is happening. It is relevant for today, but it must be spiritually understood. Even the Old Testament testifies of Jesus if we understand the types and symbols that explain its mysteries. The parables were written so that those who have the wisdom and revelation of God will understand. The Bible comes alive so to speak when revelation from the Holy Spirit teaches us the deep truths that lie within.

Also in this same village close to the church were a few poles set up with a palm leaf roof overhead. This is where the meals were prepared and we ate at a big homemade table there. The cooking was done over a fire. One night as the fire was burning bright, one of our team went out to check on the fire because we were going to have some coffee after the service. No one was out there by the fire. The person saw a poisonous snake that had been drawn by the fire and was almost bitten had not God intervened. The snake was very aggressive. The enemy will show up in various ways to destroy what God is doing. This was a snake that could have just been there naturally. If it is something that is done using witchcraft, then God shows us in the spirit and we are warned. There is nothing to fear because God will cause us to discern and warn us of impending danger as we keep sensitive to His Spirit. If God did not guide me and cause me to understand spiritual things, I would not ever know why things happened or what was happening. I have seen too many times that even insects and animals can be under demonic influence. When things act strangely or are unnaturally aggressive, my spirit senses that there is more to what is happening that I see in the natural. I listen to the still, small voice of my spirit to hear what God is telling me about the situation. Spiritual things are hard to explain especially to those who have no understanding of such. The spiritual realm is very active and one must be alert to discern.

On another occasion in another larger and more modern village, days down the river from Iquitos, I again had opportunity to see the protection of God. The team I was with in this village stayed in a hotel with decent accommodations. I had a fan, but no electricity because the generator would not work in the village. The shower worked and was a real blessing to me. It was a wonderful treat for me to have a private shower and be really clean. The heat never let us quit perspiring, but one could change sweat from time to time with a shower! The bed was comfortable and the place was reasonably clean. There has to be so much chemical placed on the floor to control the insect infestations. The floors were made of cement and very slippery and wet with the chemical.

The day after we moved into the hotel, a shaman from Brazil moved in next door to us. He was in the room between the pastor and me. He knew that we were doing services in the village and this was a threat to his work there among the people. Shamans are similar to witchdoctors and also put curses on things for evil. The next morning when I woke up and daylight allowed me to see, I viewed three very huge spiders on the wall. I had never seen spiders so big. I could not see in the dark the night before so they must have been there for a while. All the while I slept God protected me from their bite. I am glad I serve a God who looks out for His children. The spiders jumped more than crawled. I tried to take a picture of them, but they moved too fast. I tried to kill them with my shoe, but to no avail. One went behind the bed and so I just got ready for the day and went to the conference where I was preaching. I mentioned it to the hotel manager and he said he would exterminate them before I got back.

The pastor told me that day that he had problems too and it was because of the shaman who stayed in that hotel. Again I was realizing that the spirit world was trying to destroy what God was doing. It takes spiritual warfare prayer to repel the works of darkness that want to distract us and give us fear. I refuse to fear because fear is not from God and my enemy is not the spiders, but the spirit behind the spiders. The presence of God was in my room and the anointing destroyed the works of the enemy. I always thank God for His faithfulness to me and I trust Him with my life. I believe no deadly thing will harm me if I surrender to the Lord and am in His will. I am not foolish with my calling from God and rely on His direction when I am doing His work.

Whether it is snakes, spiders, ants or whatever that try to give me fear, God will keep me safe and at peace. I know that trials will come, yet I will count it all joy to serve Him in that jungle. The people are starting to see that God is not a God who does evil. He is different than the witchdoctors and shamans. He is more powerful than the devil and He has a plan for each life to be all that He created it to be. He brings peace and joy into people's hearts because He gives them hope and purpose. He is faithful to show all who seek Him the revelation and truth of His Word. He loves unconditionally and dwells in the hearts of mankind.

Father, teach us to discern when you are showing us things. Teach us to know good from evil that we be not deceived. Keep our feet on straight paths that we would not wander out of your will and purpose for us. Help us to listen carefully to the voice of your spirit warning us of impending danger. Thank you for your faithfulness to protect us even when we do not realize it is you. Bless the words of our mouths and the works of our hands that we would only encourage and strengthen through them. Let our hearts not fear or doubt your ability to keep us in the face of danger. We give you the glory. Amen.

Many years I have gone to the villages in the jungle and have seen the miracles and love of God change lives. I have seen that people are waiting for the truth and the evidence that there is a God who cares for them. I have seen pastors who cry out in prayer for help and then God sends someone to them from another country. I have seen God's protection and provision in every situation. I have seen progress in the natural and progress in the spiritual maturity of the believers also. I have seen terrorists become Christians and be leaders in the church that they tried to destroy. I have seen revelations of what God is doing in the hearts and lives of mankind to bring them into their destinies. My faith in God has grown and my heart has been humbled by the love that He has for the people in the far corners of the world. I have walked in supernatural anointings that only came from God to do signs, wonders and miracles to set people free. I have seen that God is alive and powerful to bring life and happiness in the worst possible conditions. I will continually go where He sends me to do what He wants me to do whatever the cost. My love for God and his people will move me to lay my life down for the sake of the gospel so that He receives all the glory and honor and praise because He is worthy of it all. It is a privilege to go in His name and declare that His Kingdom has come. He will continually call us to take up our cross and follow Him. What else would we rather do?

CHAPTER 15

God Is Faithful

ONE BOAT TRIP out of the main port at Iquitos was full of divine spiritual connections. I took a few pastors and leaders with me on one of the best launches I had ever been on. It was a triple decker and we had a small room with bunk beds in it where the women slept. We kept most of the suitcases and supplies under the beds so all was safe. I wanted so badly to have a lady pastor, who lived in a village down the river eight hours, to be with us. We tried to contact her by radio, but to no avail. She was in the city of Iquitos and tried to contact us, but we had already left for the boat. I knew we would pass her village in the middle of the night, but did not have any hope to see her because we could not stop there or we would not make boat connections in a city on another river about three days ahead.

We were all tired and sleeping in our beds in the camarote (little room with bunks). The guys were in the hammocks sleeping. We were on the top floor and close to the front so the location was great. The pastor's son was in the hammock close to the stairs leading to the lower decks. I woke up in the middle of the night feeling like my pastor friend, that I wanted to go along with us, was very near. I thought maybe we were close to her village, which we were. I got up and went out to the side of the boat to see if I could see any lights anywhere. I saw nothing but the blackness of the jungle and heard only the water flowing out in back of the boat as we cruised down river. I went back to my bed, but I felt in my spirit that my friend was really close by. I was just about asleep again, when a knock came at the door. The pastor's son was awake in the night and up the stairs came my pastor friend to tell

155

the captain to stop at her village and let her off. He called out to her and surprised her that he was there. He brought her to my room and she was really surprised when she saw I was there on the boat. She was on the same boat we were, but was on the first deck. She WAS near and I picked her up in my spirit because we are so knit together spiritually if you can understand that. It is like a David/Jonathon relationship from the Bible. We were one in the spirit of the Lord. We were so glad to see each other again. It has been a year since I last saw her. I usually get to see her either in the city or at her village.

We told her we were going to a leadership conference in San Lorenzo, but first we had to make a connection at Yurimaguas. There is a fork where two rivers meet and one village is on one river and the other is on another. I asked her if she could go with us at such short notice. I told her I would take care of her costs. She said she would come with us, but she had to stop at her village to drop off the supplies she bought in the city and tell her mother that she would be gone for a few days with us. Her mother asked who she would be with and she said, Georgia. Her mother was so pleased and said that she would be in good hands. I loved the people in that village. It was the first village I ever went to on the rivers and since then I have returned several times. So within a few minutes she was back on the boat with her little bundle of clothes and her tent. She had never been to the place where we were going. It was three days from her village. She would have many new and exciting experiences in Yurimaguas as I would.

When I leave the city of Iquitos to go on a river trip, I usually have no connection with the outside world. In Iquitos I have access to the internet, but where it is primitive, there is no communication. My husband can not hear from me until I return to the city which may be two or three weeks later. He just has to trust God that I am all right and I must do the same with him and the rest of my family. It is hard to be isolated in this way and I pray hard that God protects all my family while I am gone. He has never failed me yet and I know He never will. I have peace when I go because I am in the perfect timing and will of God. My mind does not override the peace in my spirit that is put there by God. I choose not to fear, but instead trust God to give me any instructions of what to do.

When we got to Yurimaguas we had to change boats and then return back to the fork in the river and take the other river over to San Lorenzo for the conference. We had a couple of days leeway because we left earlier to leave time for delays if there were any. There always are delays on the boat trips because there are so many unknowns that enter into the picture. Well, we had a delay there in Yurimaguas, a big delay. We stayed at a hotel that was on the river bank so we could see the boat when it came in. We did not see the boat come in as two days passed going on three. The conference was now starting and still no boat to get there with. I was putting everyone up in two rooms in the hotel and feeding them in restaurants. Things were pretty cheap way back there in the jungle. Some of the group had never had an opportunity to stay in a hotel and have a real shower before. The town we were in was fairly modern with hotels and stores and would you believe an internet café or two. There were men working with the oil rigs that had to contact the outside world so there was a satellite that gave access for phones and internet. I was able to e-mail my husband and tell him where I was and what was happening. He looked up some information on the city on our home computer and knew all about the place. I told him I would not be able to contact him once I left that town. While in this town, the Lord spoke to my pastor friend and she felt that the Lord was calling her to start a church in this city. She had several churches that she had started in other smaller places, but she found a piece of land that she prayed over and declared hers for a new church to be built there some day. God would do it in His time. One never knows the divine connections that come about through the leading of the Spirit until they happen. There is no need to worry or strive. God will lead each one into his or her destiny as he or she obeys His voice. The Word says that God directs our paths and He does. (Proverbs 3:6)

I did not know how I would get to the conference that was

starting that evening. We were sitting on the veranda of the hotel eating when the pastor just casually says to us, "I checked at a little airport here and there is a plane leaving in one hour. It is a five passenger airplane flying directly to San Lorenzo and it has two seats left on it." He asked me if we could afford to take it and be at the conference in good time. I said of course and quickly packed my things and we went to the plane and left. The others had to wait for a boat that would take two days to travel to San Lorenzo once it ever arrived. The plane trip would take forty minutes.

I sat up front with the pilot in the plane and had the most wonderful experience seeing the rivers from a perfect height in the plane. The sky was clear and I could take great pictures of the rivers. I had studied my map so I knew where we were and was able to see the different rivers that entered the main channels. We landed on just a small piece of land and the children ran out to meet the plane. It dropped us all off and took off to somewhere else. There was no airport, just a landing strip of sorts. The church was very close to where we landed and they were so glad to see us. They did not know me, so I was introduced to everyone. We went to another hotel there and got ready for the evening service. Everyone was excited and God had given me a good message for that night. The rest of the group did not arrive until two days later. They took such a small, crowded boat that it hardly allowed them room to move around. There may not even have been space to get to a bathroom if there was one! I would have never made it on that boat with my size. God spared me and let me take a plane that arrived quickly. I praised God for His goodness to His servant.

There was a generator in the town so there was electricity and we even had an electronic keyboard for the worship time. The Lord was really pampering me, I thought, after some of the places I had ministered in. This was not roughing it at all for me. If I had a private bathroom, I was in glory. There were assortments of bugs, of course, in the room, but such is jungle life.

At my church in Florida, I had received much prophetic word concerning this trip. God knew exactly what would happen and used people to speak to me of prophetic acts that I would do. These are acts that mean something spiritually for the situation at hand. Someone gave me some salt to throw into the rivers that would heal all the land the rivers touched from demonic influences so that the gospel could be preached successfully in those places. I waited on the Lord for the timing and place to do that. It happened on the last day as we were leaving this town deep in the jungle. The pastor and I prayed and then spoke prophetically of the healing to the people's hearts and lives.

In a vision, the Lord showed me holding a lit sword. I was going to use it to dispel the darkness that would be there. I bought a big, plastic sword from the United States that was able to give light a good distance away. It was full of tiny lights and was just what I needed. I did not know when I would use it, but I brought it all the way on the boat and just kept it in my room until God said to take it somewhere. One night I felt to take it to the evening service at the church there in San Lorenzo. We had electricity each evening up to that point and I didn't know why this was the night, but I obeyed the Holy Spirit and took it in a duffle bag I had brought. No one knew it was there. I arrived early to the church and the musicians were playing their instruments as the people began to arrive. All of a sudden all of the village went dark. The generator malfunctioned or ran out of gas or something. There was no light anywhere. I now knew that it was time to take out the sword and hold it up high and even dance with it in my hand. When the sword came out and lit up, the people could not believe it. God knew that this very thing would happen and told me to bring my sword. He is so faithful. The light from the sword lit up the church from the front to the back. Soon there were candles and flashlights to give more light. As I danced with that sword in the front of the church, I knew that demonic strongholds were being broken and the devil would not destroy the meetings. We had a wonderful time of freedom in the Spirit and much dancing unto the Lord occurred. The dancing had been thought of as evil before because the witchdoctors did it. The people did not realize that God ordained His church to dance even in the Scriptures. The

Psalms are full of scriptures about dancing. When it is not sensual or devilish, but unto the Lord in praise, God is pleased. It is just one of the expressions of worship mentioned in the Word. There are many if we want to know about them. We had no electricity in the following evening meetings except that we rented a small generator that gave the church electricity for two hours a night. The fuel was costly, but God provided for it all. The meetings went for hours into the night. The people did not want to leave when the anointing was setting them free. We were tired, but filled with joy and peace.

We had a night when we had a wedding for several of those wanting to get married. In the jungle, the people really do not have any weddings. They just live together and have children and, therefore, they are married. That is the native way. There are no records of marriage nor births nor deaths in many villages. Some villages do not even have paper to record anything on. One really does not even know what day it is or the date of any event that happens. Just recently some places are starting to record important information. We had a full course chicken dinner served late at night with no lights except the sword, candles and a flashlight or two. We served over 300 people who all sat in the church and plates were brought to them. The wedding was very fun to watch and I took many pictures. I bought ingredients for the wedding cake and the ladies of the church decorated it just beautifully. The decorations were pink toilet paper streamers that served nicely as they hung from the rafters. This church had a tin roof, but it had a dirt floor. That floor would be made of concrete some year when there was money for it. Materials could be bought in the town, that was good sized for the jungle. Some villages have thousands of people and are located in major travel routes. Most villages are from one or two hundred people to five hundred people.

I was able to eat boiled ants and fried caterpillar type worms. The fruit was delicious. Nothing I ate made me in the least bit sick. I felt great when I was in the jungle with those wonderful people. I really do love them and wish I could be with them more. There is so much more I want to see before God says that my work is done there. I know He will tell me that some day. Until then, I will return and do His work as He directs. I want to give others an opportunity to go with me too if God permits. I feel it is important to train and equip others who have a calling to those far away primitive places.

I have only hit a few highlights of some of these trips. We often baptized many, many people in the river. When they would come up out of the water, I anointed their feet with oil as another prophetic act to commission them to spread the good news of the gospel to others everywhere they walked. The Bible says that our feet are to be shod with the gospel of peace as part of the armor God has given us. (Ephesians 6:15) Everywhere we walk we can bring the peace of God into the hearts of mankind. Peace is a condition of the heart and not absence of war like I stated in another chapter.

Sometimes we would have workshops at the conferences to teach people how to play guitar and lead worship. Sometimes we would train the people in the church to go out and evangelize their own village. We provided them with tracts and many received the Lord as their personal Savior and were invited to the church. At other times, we had prophetic teaching and training to better prepare those operating in the revelatory gifts. The freedom in the Sprit is necessary for the spiritual gifts to function. There was teaching on deliverance from demonic influences and strongholds. We taught them how to stay firm on the Word of God to discipline their minds against deception from other evil influences. Some workshops were even able to teach sewing and hair cutting. At times we carried sewing machines on the boats to places where there would be electricity. Patterns were made out of newspaper and we purchased cloth and sewing supplies in the city. The women were thrilled with learning these trades.

Little by little the people learned and were able to teach others. If we all work together and share what we know how to do, all will be blessed. Each person has something to share and needs to be encouraged to try and be given an opportunity to do something new.

There are some pastors who are like sons to me. I have become a spiritual mother, so to speak, training them in the apostolic and prophetic anointings. They need guidance and teaching to keep them from getting frustrated with the callings God has placed in their lives. They face many temptations and trials. They get lonely and feel isolated at times. Many times they have to be away from home and leave their wives and children for long periods of time. The trips on the rivers to visit the churches take many days and there is no communication for weeks sometimes. All is very hard for us to imagine. We usually call home and check to see if everyone is all right every day when we are separated from our families for ministry reasons. This is where faith is really tested and every person must learn to keep focused and tuned into the spiritual voice of God. It is walking in the Spirit in such a way that the worries and fears of what could happen do not even enter the mind. God is in control and knows just what will happen in our lives. This is so comforting to understand when I have to rely totally on His wisdom and knowledge. Whatever challenge I have to face, I face it with faith in God and trust Him for the outcome. I can say that He has never failed me yet, and I know He never will if I stay in his perfect plan for my life and ministry.

Over the years my husband and I have traveled to different areas of the country of Peru to see ancient Inca cultures and Pre-Inca cultures. The ruins fascinated me since I studied some of these in my education for becoming a Spanish teacher. I learned more culture than I had ever known from books. Of course, these cultures were founded on idolatry worshipping sun gods, volcano gods, sky, sea, and earth gods, etc. The cultures also believed and practiced human sacrifice. These ancient people of several centuries ago were very skilled in gold-working and other precious metals. They made everything they needed from what the ground produced or was found in the sea. Some cultures were skilled in art and it was evident as one would look at the detailed drawings on textiles, pottery, and other artifacts. Some cultures were not artistic, working with mostly geometric designs, but were very knowledgeable in science and mathematics. Many giftings were seen in various cultures and no one really knows where they learned all these things. Some think that Egypt taught them centuries ago and they migrated to the Americas. Many similarities are found in certain styles of art and architecture. I would like to study more along this area some day when I have time, which probably will never happen!

There are still sacrificial altars being used by offshoots from Inca peoples. There are mostly animal sacrifices being made to their idols to appease these gods.

The truth of the gospel of Jesus Christ is so needed in the hearts of the people who have a dead, hopeless religion. Little by little lives are being changed to worship the one true and living God. The power of God is greater than any witchcraft or voodoo. There are power struggles in the unseen spiritual realm that most people never even realize are there. Spiritual darkness is prevalent all over this earth. People do not see clearly what takes place in the demonic realm. Only by the Holy Spirit will anyone ever understand that the devil is real, but Jesus Christ is truly alive and doing wonders to defeat the works of the evil one. The Christian has authority and power over principalities and powers of darkness. Jesus came to be the Light of the World and open our spiritual eyes to see that He has a plan for our lives to bring us hope and freedom. All of the power of the enemy was put under Jesus' feet when he died on the cross for our sins, and rose again victorious over death and the grave. He comes to give life more abundantly while the devil comes to steal, kill and destroy. Our hope must be in a living God who will teach us truth that we may walk in victory.

I pray that as years go by, many missionaries will bring the light of the Gospel to these people who live in fear and spiritual darkness. We all will spend eternity in either heaven or hell. The choice is ours, but someone must teach and preach the truth to everyone who does not know Jesus as Lord and Savior.

CHAPTER 16

Closing Statement

WHAT IS CALLING your name? Is it another nation and culture or is it your neighborhood? Are you even aware that God has a plan for your life and wants you to follow Him into your destiny. He has surely called you into a walk with Him in faith and surrender. He knew when you would be born and He knows when you will die. He put special callings inside you when you were brought into this world. These special callings are shaping your future in ways you may not even understand.

Do you ever ask yourself why you want to do what you do? Why you want to live where you live? What is it that makes you who you are? It was God that put all that in you so that you would be a creation that was uniquely designed by the Master for purpose and destiny in His Kingdom. He wants you to be His child and grow and mature to have wisdom and understanding of all that He has for you. You were not an accident nor were you a mistake. You are here on this earth for such a time as this.

The inner desires of our hearts are the very credentials for the ministries that God has ordained for us to do. He is drawing us by His Spirit into a spiritual relationship that can only be realized as we surrender our hearts and lives to Him. We can trust Him by faith that His Word is truth. He can never lie nor go back on His Word. He will always take us into our destiny the easiest way we will go. When we resist and rebel, He will still work in our lives to accomplish His purpose for us. He never forces us to do or be anything. He gently leads us and asks us to follow Him. It will mean that we die to our own selfish desires and agree to let

165

Him take us forward changing us into His image as we obey His Word and understand His heart.

There is a heavenly perspective that we must have. This earth is only a temporary place that God has chosen to perfect us. All of life will transform us into His image if we will cooperate with the Holy Spirit and yield our will to His. Jesus has said that He began a good work in us and will finish it if we will allow Him to do it. His purpose is higher than ours and His ways are the best and only ways to live life in victory and peace.

As you read this book, please understand that it was only because I trusted God with my life and believed His Word was true that I went forward into my destiny of being a teacher and a missionary. Many hard and complicated events took place as I matured and reached forward into what God had for me. The hope and calling within me propelled me forward by faith with a joy that I cannot explain. To serve my Lord and be obedient to His will was my highest privilege as we labored together in every area of ministry. I know it was His grace and anointing that did the work, but I made myself available and flexible that He could use me. As my life unfolded, His will for me became more clear. As I saw Him at work in my life, I loved and trusted Him more. With each step I took towards my destiny, I realized that the supernatural realm was absolutely more real than even the natural, physical world I lived in on this earth. The eternal perspective is a greater insight to me than any amount of knowledge received here in my earthly mind and understanding.

The joy set before me and the treasure of wisdom I have in Jesus will mold me into the image that He has called me to have. My eyes are focused on Him and His direction for me. All that I must experience in this life will be worth everything so I can be a praise and blessing to my King. I do not want to leave one thing undone that He has ordained for me to do. I want to be a good and faithful servant of the most high God of heaven and earth and spend all eternity learning the mysteries of the Godhead. My days are numbered by Him and He will do all in His time that He may be glorified in my service to Him. May God be praised.

166

Contact Georgia Egge or order more copies of this book at

TATE PUBLISHING, LLC

127 East Trade Center Terrace
Mustang, Oklahoma 73064

(888) 361 - 9473

TATE PUBLISHING, LLC

www.tatepublishing.com